THE GREAT DANE HANDBOOK

by
Mary J. McCracken

OTR Publications
Centreville, AL

ISBN 0-940269-08-2

Library of Congress Cataloging-in-Publication Data

McCracken, Mary J., 1955-
         The Great Dane handbook / by Mary J. McCracken.
                    p.   cm.
ISBN 0-940269-08-2
1. Great Danes.   I. Title
SF429.G7M38   1995
636.7 ' 3--dc20   95-38576
                                                   CIP

OTR PUBLICATIONS
P.O. Box 481
Centreville, AL 35042

Dedication

To Zeus and Dozer,

the spirit behind these words...

and to Michael,

whose love and support made this book possible

Front Cover Photo: Daynakin's I'm A Rolling Thunder CDX, TD, Can. CD, TD, U-CD, WDX, HC, TDI and Am. & Can. Ch. and Can. O.T. Ch. Danehaven's Rolling Thunder UDT, Can. UDTDX, WDX, HC, U-CDX, TDI owned by Marta Brock, Rolling Thunder Danes, Olympia, Washington

Back Cover Photo: Walhalla's Liebestraum CD, CGC owned by Chris and Henry Bredenkamp, Siegreich Danes, Burleson, Texas

Frontispiece: Ch. Travis Lincoln owned by Sandy Britts (Des'Dany Danes) and Clare Lincoln (Lincoln Danes), Puyallup, Washington

Contents Page: A Boston female owned by Jennie Weber and bred by Carol Beene, Crickhollow Danes, Denton, Texas

Section I: Am. & Can. Ch. and Can. O.T. Ch. Danehaven's Rolling Thunder UDT, Can. UDTDX, WDX, HC, U-CDX, TDI; Daynakin's I'm A Rolling Thunder CDX, TD, Can. CD, TD, U-CD, WDX, HC, TDI; Can. Ch. Paquestone's V. Rolling Thunder CDX, TD, Can. CDX, TD, U-CD, ASCA CD, WD, TDI owned by Marta Brock, Rolling Thunder Danes, Olympia, Washington

Section II: Future Ch. Brier's Duesenberg V. Hauer and Hauerdane's Fancy Fox of Brier at five weeks of age. Bred by Beverly Hauer and Karen Lindsay, Hauerdane, Alpine, California

Section III: Brett's Instanz V. Siegreich CDX, TDI and Siegreich's Impulsiv Ersatz CD with their Min Pin friend. Owned by Chris and Henry Bredenkamp, Siegreich Danes, Burleson, Texas

Section IV: Ch. Mei-Ling's Jordon Ultimo CDX, CGC, TT, owned by Jill Zondervan, San Jose, California

CONTENTS

SECTION TWO: BRINGING UP BABY

SECTION III: THE HEALTH OF YOUR DANE

37. Competition, Exercise and Just Plain Fun   205

Swimming • Junior Handling • Hiking • Agility • Bicycling •
Fun Runs • Frisbee • Flyball • Tracking • Carting •
Car Travel • Fun and Games

APPENDICES

FOREWORD

In 1978, I began my odyssey with the Great Dane. As a veterinary technician, I worked closely with most breeds on a daily basis. What attracted me to the Dane was the breed's temperament. Without exception, the Danes visiting the clinic were stable and friendly. I wanted to become active in obedience and tracking and the size, dignity and intelligence of the breed appealed to me. The decision to purchase a Dane was an easy one.

I have never regretted my decision. Over the past two decades, I have had many triumphs, my share of failures and many very memorable moments. Along the way, I've met a lot of wonderful people. Many people, even Dane owners, are unaware of how much the breed has to offer. Showing a Dane to a breed championship is an exhilarating accomplishment, but not all Danes are born with the conformation to achieve this title. What then is there for *every* Dane and his owner? The answer can be found in the pages of Mary McCracken's fun new book. The Dane is a member of the Working Group, and rightly so. This book introduces the Dane owner to many of the sports and games which dogs and their owners can enjoy together. It is a book long overdue, covering activities too often overlooked by the majority of Dane breeders and owners. It is disappointing indeed that the Dane, the "King of Dogs," has never taken its rightful place among the ranks of top working breeds. This is due, in part, to a historical lack of interest, among Dane fanciers, in the dog sports, but also because there has never before been a book like this to educate the Dane owner to the numerous options available. Hopefully, in the future, we will see many more Danes participating in tracking, obedience, flyball, agility, Frisbee competitions and other sports and games.

It was an honor to be asked to write the foreword for this important book. Over the years, I've tried to take advantage of every opportunity to promote the Dane as a working/sport dog. I have tried to help my dogs reach their full potential, and I think this book will help others to do the same. Nothing can compare, in my opinion, to the thrill of working closely with your dog—watching him learn, achieve, triumph and enjoy himself. It was my deepest honor and pleasure to have worked with Can. OTCH, Am/ Can. Ch. Danehaven's Rolling Thunder, UDT, Can. UDTDX, WDX, U-CDX, HC, TDI. He was just one of the many Danes I have loved, over the years, but undeniably the one dog who best represented the breed as a working/sport dog. I found, and I think other Dane owners will find this book invaluable, no matter what level you aspire to reach. Even if you simply plan to take your dog into the back yard and enjoy a few doggie games together, this book will open new horizons of enjoyment for you and your special friend.

Marta Brock

ACKNOWLEDGEMENTS

Grateful thanks to Marta Brock and Linda Arndt for their contributions; to all the breeders and Dane owners who offered both photographs and advice; to my editor, Cathy J. Flamholtz, for making this a better book; to Drs. Deschamps and Coleman for teaching me so much and taking such wonderful care of my dogs; to the Great Dane Club of Greater Houston for their welcome support; to Susan Barney and "Ox," for introducing me to the breed; and to my family, for the encouragement and faith that allowed me to write this book.

SECTION I

BEFORE YOU ADOPT A GREAT DANE

Both children and dogs require love, patience and commitment. Jackson Garcia, of Pasadena, Texas, and Dagmar's Sohni are already best friends.

1

SHOULD YOU OWN A DOG?

Before you carry home that warm, sweet bundle of fur—stop! Think long and hard. Life is about to change—for you, the others in your household and the innocent puppy who will soon be the dog you created. Sit down with the family and answer these questions honestly.

1. Are you committed to a relationship with your dog that will last for its lifetime? A dog bonds quickly and forever to the family. You are its pack and its life. The dog you raise with love and patience will never betray you. To experience your betrayal would be heartbreaking—even devastating. Can you say with conviction: "This dog will be part of my family through training problems, illness, financial difficulties and chewed furniture—till death do us part"? Great! You're an excellent candidate to own a dog.

2. Can you afford a dog? In today's difficult economic times, many of us are struggling. Owning a dog can be very expensive. The initial purchase cost is only the beginning. Phone a local vet and ask what you can expect to spend for vaccinations, checkups and other preventive care for a year. What will it cost for spaying or neutering? Already you see that even the bare necessities of veterinary care will affect your bank account, and those amounts can increase dramatically if your dog becomes ill or is injured. You will need at least basic obedience classes for your dog. Check with

trainers or dog clubs in your area for recommendations and expected costs. Will you handle grooming chores at home? If not, a quick call to a groomer will give you another expense to add to your list. Now drop by your local pet store. Note the costs of quality food, dishes, collars, leashes, beds, crates, toys, grooming tools and other accessories. If you plan to participate in dog-related activities, such as conformation, obedience showing, flyball, etc., you can expect to spend even more—possibly much more. For those of us who adore dogs and feel that life is incomplete without them, these costs are a small price to pay for love, loyalty, unconditional acceptance and just plain fun. Be honest with yourself—if you'd rather spend money on the latest computer craze, hot new clothes or weekend getaways, please don't get a dog.

With proper care and attention, your Dane puppy will become a life-long friend. This is Lucky Ladd Jazz of Flam'g Oak, owned by Janice and Leonard Jerue, Dickinson, Texas.

3. Do you have time for a dog? Daily exercise alone will cut into your free time. Your puppy must be housebroken, fed, watered, groomed, picked up after and trained to be a good family member. She needs lots of play and affection, and quality time with you every single day. You probably intend to "find the time" somewhere. But if you are already stressed by the attempt to fit everything into your daily schedule, adding a dog to your life will

only increase the stress level. You will feel guilty and your dog will be miserable. Wait until the pace of your life slows down before adding a pet.

4. Does a dog fit into your household? Are you bothered by dog hair on your clothes or furniture? Will puppy accidents or muddy paws pose a serious threat to your beautiful home? Do you have white carpets, antique furniture, expensive knicknacks? Picture the wear and tear a dog will impose on your home. You know, having a dog is not much different than having a child—both can be time consuming, messy and troublesome. If you see the love and companionship as its own reward, and the problems outweighed by the benefits, a dog should fit quite nicely into your household.

5. What do you expect from your dog? Whatever plans and dreams you may have, she should be first and foremost a family member and companion. If your "show" dog can't cut the mustard, will you still love her? If your "watchdog" only watches the backs of her eyelids, can you live with that? Do you understand that a dog is a living creature with thoughts and feelings, not a stuffed toy for the kids or a barking burglar alarm for you?

What should you expect? A loyal friend who depends on you, makes you feel needed, and shares your life; a playmate; a best buddy who increases your feelings of security and well being; for some, even a reason to get up in the morning. Are your expectations realistic? Do you have the time, the money, the patience and the energy? Yes? Congratulations—you're about to embark on a wonderful relationship with your new canine companion!

Great Danes are great companions for children (Magic's Stairway to Heaven, bred by Linda Altomare and owned by Tom & Kathy Hinson)

...as well as adults. (Brett's Instanz V. Siegreich CDX, TDI and "Mom" Chris Bredenkamp.

2

IS A GREAT DANE THE DOG FOR YOU?

Hopefully, in Chapter one, you discovered that you're a great dog owner just waiting for a great dog. And since you're reading this book, you're obviously interested in the giant breeds, especially the oh-so elegant Great Dane. Proceed with caution—this wonderful dog is not for everyone.

Your dog will be both a joy and a responsibility. The more carefully you choose your breed, the less problems you are likely to experience in your life together. You have hundreds of breeds to choose from, each with characteristics that may or may not suit your lifestyle. If you make the wrong choice, both you and the dog may be headed for trouble. If you wrongfully choose a giant breed, that trouble may be bigger than you can imagine. The well-bred, properly raised and trained giant should conjure up images of a well-behaved, friendly, awe-inspiring companion. But if poorly bred, raised or trained, you may end up with unstuffed couches, frightened neighbors and frazzled nerves. And what should have been a happy companion dog, secure in his place in the family, could instead end up a neurotic and dangerous animal, destined for the pound or euthanasia.

A Great Dane is only truly happy when with his family. He is demanding, craving love, affection and companionship. If kept in a basement or back yard, or left alone constantly, the Dane becomes ill, unhappy and destructive. He needs a committed, devoted family willing to provide quality time every day.

Should you choose a small dog, like Gidget, or a giant one, like Ch. Hope-N-Dagon's Flashy Hanna, owned by Terry Beck, of Conroe, Texas?

While he may look scary to the uninitiated, the Dane is probably not your best choice for a guard or protection dog. His very size necessitates socializing him to be a friend to man. While a Dane who loves his family will no doubt be watchful and protective, this huge dog should never be expected to decide on his own who is friend and who is foe, and how he should respond to each. Consider the consequences if he should make the wrong choice. A Dane allowed to develop aggressive, overly territorial tendencies could cause severe injury or death, possibly to a child or other innocent person. If you want a loving companion whose mere presence would deter an intruder, this may be your dog. If you're looking for round-the-clock protection, choose another breed or, better yet, buy an alarm system.

You must provide your Dane with

The Dane is alert and protective. Grayland's Socretiese of Hog Creek, owned by Susan and Herb Barney, guards his Pearland, Texas home.

plenty of space indoors and out. Start with a soft cozy bed, preferably in a room or area of his own. He needs a fenced yard, large enough to allow him to move about freely. He also won't fit into the Toyota with the kids and the groceries. You must have adequate transportation for vet visits, training sessions and family outings.

Danes love creature comforts. Ch. Hope-N-Dagon's Flashy Hanna, owned by Terry Beck, prefers a waterbed.

This breed must be well trained. If not, he'll grow into a hazard—to himself, you and others. Imagine a 150 pound dog dragging you through the neighborhood, chasing cats and jumping on children! You must be willing to patiently teach firm rules of behavior, and those rules must be enforced gently and with fairness.

He needs a carefully designed exercise routine. Too much exercise in formative periods can cause bone and growth problems; too little exercise will not provide the aerobic effect needed to allow his heart and lungs to sustain his size. A bored, underexercised dog of any breed can be destructive—a bored Dane can wreak massive havoc!

While grooming requirements for a Dane are much easier than those of many breeds, anything other than brushing can be an ordeal if he's not accustomed to the routine. He may not like the frequent nail clipping he needs to prevent painful foot problems, unless you teach him very early that it's a regular part of his life. His teeth must be brushed regularly, and he will no doubt require a bath now and then. You can expect to carry a small towel or handkerchief wherever you go, because he drools when he's excited. He may also decide to get friendly right after drinking water, in which case you'll get a bath along with the doggie kiss.

You will need adequate transportation. Terry Beck's Ch. Hope-N-Dagan's Flashy Hanna and Janice & Leonard Jerue's Ch. VZ Top Ragtime Boy V. Flam'g Oak are out for a ride in the van.

Feeding your Dane will not be economical. He requires excellent nutrition, frequent meals, and a balanced diet.

Other expenses will be greater than with smaller dogs—bigger prices for bigger dishes, crates, toys, collars, etc. Spaying and neutering, and other veterinary expenses such as medications, will be considerably higher.

While the Dane is a great companion for both children and grownups, he is just too big for infants, toddlers, the elderly or the infirm.

Your Great Dane wants to be your best friend. In return for the lavish care and devotion he requires, you'll have a strong, sensitive, ever-loyal companion. He will impress your neighbors, frighten intruders, romp with your children and stay close by your side. Not only is he big physically, he's big in heart and spirit, the epitome of courage, patience, love and loyalty. He needs and deserves a family with those same qualities in equal abundance.

3

HISTORY

It is not within the scope of this book to offer a complete and detailed history of the breed. Still, it is important that every Dane fancier have, at least, some general knowledge of the breed's background. This can provide us with many clues about the behavior of the modern Dane.

Many writers have speculated on the origin of the Great Dane. Some believe he was descended from the mighty Molossus, of Greece. Others point to his resemblance to the big game hunting dogs raised by the Assyrians. Still others contend that his likeness is portrayed on Egyptian monuments which date to 3,000 BC. And numerous scholars credit the Tibetan Mastiff as the grand-daddy of all our Mastiff-type dogs. Many breed historians tell us that the Phoenicians, those adventurous sailors who plied the waters of the Mediterranean and the Atlantic, first brought these ancient dogs to Europe.

Whatever the truth of his origin, we do know that, by Roman times, these mastiff-like dogs had become popular in Britain. The Romans were fond of the barbaric practice of pitting dogs against lions and bears, in their infamous arenas. The poor dogs destined for such "entertainment" had originally been procured from Greece. However, with the conquering of England, the Romans discovered the brawny British dogs who were reputed to be strong enough to break the neck of an ox. So taken were they with these huge dogs that they designated an official officer, the "Procurator Cynogie," to purchase dogs for baiting. He was headquartered in Winchester, which became known as the "City of Dogs."

It is the descendants of these valiant warriors who would become famous, during the Middle Ages, as big game hunters. During the 15th and 16th centuries, European forests teemed with game. Bears, wolves and large packs of wild pigs roamed freely. Huge hunting extravaganzas became the sport of choice for noblemen who took great pride in breeding horses and dogs to aid in the hunt. The number of animals slaughtered during such hunts was phenomenal. In 1559, Germany's Landsgrafen Philipp reportedly caught 1,120 wild boar and, in 1563, his tally was an astounding 2,572 wild boar killed. Duke Henry, of Braunschweig, was said to have taken 600 male dogs to a 1592 hunt!

German historians tell us that these early dogs played two roles in the hunt. Some ran as a pack, driving the boars toward the hunters until a lone animal could be

The Great Dane was once an invincible boar hunter, as this early print shows. *From the Flamholtz collection*

singled out. The strongest, bravest and most powerful of the dogs were held in reserve. These attacked the separated boar, seizing and holding him until the hunters could arrive. Approaching either on horseback or foot, the hunters then speared the animal.

Ear cropping was done during this time, but for utilitarian, rather than cosmetic, reasons. The houndy ears of the early Boarhounds were particularly vulnerable in the hunt. Boars often grabbed the hanging ears, tearing and lacerating them badly. Many a dog died from the wounds or the infection which followed.

These Boarhounds were wildly popular among German nobility, and royal kennels took great pride in the dogs they bred. The native Boarhounds were massive, powerful, tenacious and blessed with great endurance. Ever eager to improve their stock, noblemen imported dogs from England. These were longer-legged, faster and more agile, probably similar to today's Irish Wolfhound or Scottish Deerhound. By the 17th or 18th century, the importation of English dogs ceased. The improved German-bred hounds were superior in the hunt. It was the combination of these two types that produced the qualities we find in the Great Dane. Indeed, this is the period when the modern Dane began to emerge.

Gradually, the wild boars of the German forest began to decrease. Some blame it on the huge numbers killed in the hunt. Others say that a drought, in 1784 and '85, resulted in the massive death of many species of wildlife. Whatever the cause, the demise of so many wild boar had an impact on the dogs used to hunt them. No longer were the huge kennels maintained. But, the dogs still had their admirers and were still bred, though in smaller numbers.

We do not know exactly how the Great Dane acquired this name. Clearly, the dogs hail from Germany, not Denmark. These early dogs were known by a variety of names. Sometimes the labels were associated with the dogs' work, thus they were known as Bearcatcher, Harehound, Pig Catcher, Pig Killer and Butcher Dog. Sometimes they took on the names of the provinces in which they were popular. Thus, dogs from the vicinity of Ulmer became known as "Ulm" or "Ulmer" dogs, a name which was to gain wider usage. Some royals selected their biggest and most handsome dogs as "Chamber Dogs." These were decked out in elaborate collars often trimmed in gold and silver. There is one piece of evidence which does have a Danish link. A 1686 engraving, by Richard Blome, depicts a pack of 13 hounds, resembling Danes, on a wild boar hunt in Denmark.

During the mid to late 1800s, Germans became interested in dog shows. Danes were exhibited at the very first show in 1863. There were two different types within the breed, during those early years. Dogs from the northern part of Germany were said to be very large, heavy boned animals, rather short in neck, while those from the southern part of the country were lighter and more graceful in appearance. These were separated into two different classes at shows.

Finally, in 1880, the two types were united under the official name, Deutsche Dogge, or German Mastiff. Interest in the breed continued to grow and, during 1880-1890 many new people took up the breed. In 1887, more than 300 Great Danes were exhibited at a show in Stuttgart. Entries at other shows routinely topped 100. In 1888, the Deutscher Doggen Klub was formed—the first German club devoted to a single breed. The club forged a modern breed standard which called for symmetry, style and elegance. Members also declared that the Dane was the "National Dog of Germany."

These impressive dogs began to attract the attention of dog lovers outside of Germany. The first Danes were imported to America in the 1870s. A brindle dog, Juno, became the first breed champion. Born in Berlin, he was imported to the Osceola Kennels, in Osceola, Wisconsin. This kennel also holds the honor of having the second breed champion, also imported from Germany. This fawn dog, Ch. Don Caesar, topped the breed at Westminster, in 1887.

Danes were often decked out in protective clothing. *From the Flamholtz collection*

Companion of Celebrities

Beloved by all, the Dane has often hobnobbed with the rich and famous. It was a dog named Bounce who saved the life of Alexander Pope (1688-1744). This prolific British poet had a rather sad life. Crippled, as a child, from a spine deformity, Pope was an invalid. He was also shunned by much of British society. Most English had converted to the Anglican religion, but Pope remained a devout Roman Catholic. He was, therefore, excluded from the social world of his day and denied a university education. He became quite bitter and was prone to bouts of wild temper.

One night, as he lay in bed, his valet sneaked into the room, brandishing a large knife. Pope was unable to get up and screamed. The loyal Bounce bounded into the room and lunged at the man, knocking him to the floor. He stood over the valet until the other servants could arrive.

It's little wonder that Pope would immortalize the breed in his writings. He also introduced the Dane to another celebrity. The Prince of Wales was so taken with Bounce that he wanted a dog just like him. Pope would give a puppy, sired by Bounce, to the Prince.

One of the Dane's most enthusiastic supporters was Prince Otto von Bismarck, who was elected Chancellor of Germany, in 1871. His love for the breed shines brightly from the pages of his diaries, which contain numerous references to his beloved dogs. Bismarck appears to have been a very indulgent owner. His dogs were allowed to cavort freely throughout his home and any bad behavior was laughed at and viewed as a sign of their spirit and intelligence. During state dinners, Bismarck often ordered extra servings of meat and, as appalled guests looked on, he threw these portions to his dogs. Reports say that Bismarck's Danes routinely interrupted him during state

Danes as they appeared in 1800, in Sydenham Edwards' *Cynographia Brittannica. From the Flamholtz collection.*

The powerful "Danish Mastiff" pictured in an 1882 issue of *Harper's Weekly. From the Flamholtz collection.*

meetings, but were never reprimanded. Indeed, the Chancellor was said to mistrust those who showed no affection toward his dogs.

The young Prince's first dog was Ariel, a fawn, whom he received as a teenager. When he left for college, Ariel went along to keep him company.

Bismarck's favorite Dane appears to have been a large blue male, named Sultan. The two could often be seen strolling in the royal gardens. Once, Bismarck canceled a summer vacation because Sultan was ailing and he could not bear to leave him alone.

Another Bismarck Dane, Tyras, almost caused an international incident. Prime Minister Gortschakoff, of Russia, was visiting Germany and he and Bismarck became embroiled in a serious dispute. The Russian's talk became particularly animated, punctuated by aggressive gestures. Tyras, lying at Bismarck's feet, became increasingly nervous. Finally, he sprang, knocking Gortschakoff to the floor and pinning him. Indeed, Tyras became so identified with the Chancellor that news of the dog's death was treated as a major story and cabled around the world. It appears that Bismarck was depressed at the loss of his faithful friend

An early German Dane headstudy. *From the Flamholtz collection*

and the Emperor presented him with a new puppy.

It was an 80 year old Bismarck who buried his last Dane. He announced that he did not want another dog. He simply couldn't bear going through the loss of another Dane. "I firmly believe that I shall see my dogs...again in heaven," he wrote in his diary.

William Cody, alias "Buffalo Bill," was to be a life-long fancier of the breed. Turk, a black Dane, was the constant companion and protector of Bill and his four sisters. Indeed, he is said to have saved the life of young Bill's sisters from a panther attack. Supposedly, when he saw the panther, the dog dug a hole, pulled the girls into it and covered it with leaves. As the animal attacked, Turk defended them. Even though he was wounded, Turk kept the panther at bay until Bill arrived and shot him.

Sadly, Turk was bitten by a rabid dog and had to be destroyed. We know, however, that Buffalo Bill remained fond of the breed. A Dane toured with him in his famed Wild West show.

This drawing of "Flora," owned by Herr Wuster, appeared in Vero Shaw's *The Illustrated Book of the Dog,* **published in 1879-81.**

The German World War I flying ace, Manfred von Richthofen, better known as the Red Baron, was also a Dane fancier. Credited with shooting down 80 Allied planes, Richthofen became a German national hero. A Dane could often be seen occupying the passenger seat of his famed red Fokker triplane.

Star of the Big Screen

Al Jolson (1886-1950) was the first star to appear in a movie with a Dane. The star of burlesque, minstrel shows and vaudeville earned world wide fame when he headed to Hollywood, in the 1920s, to star in films. A Dane, named Baron Content, appeared with him in *Big Boy.* Owned by

Today's Great Dane combines strength and elegance, as demonstrated by Specialty and Best in Show winner Ch. Travis Lincoln owned by Sandy Britts and Clare Lincoln.

Colonel Ferguson, of Estid Kennels, Baron was the first Great Dane seen in a talking picture.

In the intervening 60 years, Danes have appeared in numerous movies, television shows, videos and commercials. Many Dane lovers include in their video collections copies of such Disney fare as *Swiss Family Robinson* and *The Ugly Dachshund*. Elvis Presley's *Live a Little, Love a Little* is also popular. In more recent years, a Dane joined Tom Hanks in *The 'Burbs* and strolled with Michael J. Fox in *For Love or Money*. This is but a small sampling of the breed's movie credits.

Danes have also appeared in episodes of many television shows. They have been featured on *Bewitched*, *The Bob Newhart Show* and, most recently, *Walker, Texas Ranger*. A harlequin appears in a rock video, by Soundgarden, called *Black Hole Sun*.

While the looks and temperament of this magnificent animal have been refined over the years, the Great Dane remains a working dog as well as a companion. He is a strong dog, requiring a strong master. Anyone without at least equal intelligence need not apply for his respect and allegiance.

Due to his tremendous size and elegance, the Great Dane is referred to as "The Apollo of Dogs." His excellent temperament has also earned him the moniker "Continental Gentleman." Whatever we choose to call him, his greatness is never in dispute.

"The Fridge," better known as Ch. Von Shrado's I'm A Knock Out, is an imposing fawn male. This outstanding male is owned by Jim and Sandy Hann, Von Shrado Great Danes, Pikeville, North Carolina.

4

PHYSICAL DESCRIPTION

    One of the giant breeds, the male Dane stands a minimum of 30" tall at the withers, the bitch a minimum of 28". Most are quite a bit taller—36" is not unusual. Still, it's important that each dog be well proportioned for the height he or she carries. The average weight is 120 to 150 pounds. To say the least, a Great Dane is an imposing sight. Still, there is nothing coarse about this dog. He is powerful and elegant, with smooth muscles rippling as he moves.

    The coat is short, smooth and thick, with a healthy gloss. The accepted colors in the AKC show ring are fawn, brindle, black, blue and harlequin. Fawn Danes should be light to deep golden yellow with a deep black mask. Brindles have a fawn base color with strong black across stripes, and preferably a deep black mask. Blue should be pure steel blue, and black a glossy black. Harlequin Danes have a white base color with irregular black torn patches. The patches should be well distributed over the body, not too large and not too small. A pure white neck is preferred.

    Breeding a "correct" harlequin can be a difficult task. Most harlequin-bred litters contain puppies which do not show the prescribed patterning. A "Boston" coloration is often produced from harlequin breedings. The Boston is black and white in a pattern resembling that of a Boston Terrier. The Boston pattern is accepted in both Europe and Canada, and may soon be eligible for AKC showing. This pattern may also be referred to as "mantled."

    The merle coloration is also produced from harlequin breedings. The base color is usually a blue-gray, with black markings. The look is very unusual and striking. A merle Dane makes a perfectly wonderful pet, and is certainly an attention-getter with his large size and odd coloring. However, merle Danes should never be bred. Danes of this coloration can possess a "lethal" gene which does not affect the health of the dog itself, but may affect the health of puppies produced by the merle. Problems seen include brain damage, blindness and deafness. Your merle companion Dane should definitely be spayed or neutered.

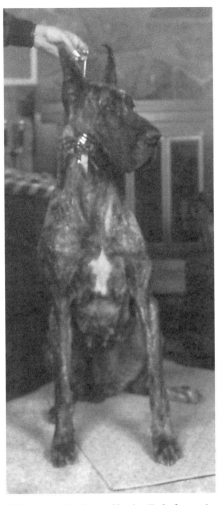

This lovely brindle is Brinlawn's Good Stuff for DD, owned by Darthy Davis, Dee Dee Danes, Coal Township, Pennsylvania. *(A. Rick Harner photo)*

There are other colors and varieties occasionally seen, such as solid white, white with fawn or brindle patches, or Boston patterns with blue or another color replacing the black. While they may be beautiful dogs, this is a sure sign that the breeder either does not know or does not care about proper breeding principles and genetics (See Breeders Color Code, Appendix B).

The Great Dane is a square dog, with an expressive rectangular head, a deep muzzle and square jaw. The eyes are of medium size, deep set

with an almond shape. While harlequins may have blue or odd eyes (one brown, one blue or even brown-blue "spotted"), dark brown is preferred on all Danes. The expression should be lively and intelligent. The nose is usually black, but may be blue-black in blue Danes and black-spotted in the harlequin. The teeth close in a scissors bite. Natural ears should be medium in size, high set and folded forward close to the cheeks. Many Danes have cropped ears, which are carried uniformly erect. Ear size should be proportionate to the size of the head. The neck is long, well arched and muscular. The broad powerful chest is set off by a tucked up abdomen. The withers slope smoothly into a short level back; the loin is broad. The tail is long and tapered, usually carried in a slight curve. Feet should be round and compact with well-arched toes. Nails are kept short.

A lovely blue female from Alice Haynes' Pappy Jack Danes, in Medford, New York.

Both the forequarters and hindquarters should be muscular and strong. The natural gait of the Great Dane is a trot. The dog should move with long, easy strides and demonstrate much strength and power of movement. When gaiting, the backline should appear level and parallel to the ground. Overall, the look of the Dane is distinguished and noble, truly "The Apollo of Dogs."

37

Natural-eared harlequins, Siegreich's Amstel V. Nahallac CDX, CGC and Walhalla's Liebestraum CD, CGC, are owned by Chris and Henry Bredenkamp, Siegreich Danes, Burleson, Texas.

The impressive black Ch. Magic's First Symphony, owned by Linda and Mike Altomare, Magic Manor Danes, Hubbard, Ohio.

Ranger, owned by Gay Hughes, of Carmi, Illinois, shows the Boston markings.

Danes live well in pairs. These devoted friends are Am. & Can. Ch. and Can. O.T. Ch. Danehaven's Rolling Thunder UDT, Can. UDTDX, WDX, HC, U-CDX, TDI and Daynakin's I'm A Rolling Thunder CDX, TD, Can. CD, TD, U-CD, WDX, HC TDI, owned by Marta Brock, Rolling Thunder Danes, Olympia, Washington.

5

PERSONALITY AND TEMPERAMENT

Every dog is different, but there are many characteristics you can expect simply because your Dane is a dog, and still others because your dog is a Dane! In other words, a Great Dane is first and foremost a canine, and will demonstrate canine behaviors handed down by his wolf ancestors. But like every breed, the Dane has certain attributes that have been purposely bred in and refined over the years. And of course, each Dane will have his own little ways that are his and his alone. This individual behavior stems from a variety of sources. Some traits are inherited from the parents, others influenced by the pup's early life with the breeder and his littermates. Many of the characteristics he demonstrates as an adult will be learned behaviors from experience and training. That means that a lot of what your Dane turns out to be is up to you!

Dogs are pack animals, adaptable and social. This very pack behavior makes them companionable with man, and they readily accept the human family as their pack. They function as part of the pack, often ready to defend their home and lifestyle.

The Great Dane is truly a lover of home, family and the comfortable life. He has a stable temperament and a sweet attitude. This dog may be big and strong, but he's also sensitive and he needs you. While other breeds are busy sneaking under the fence or jumping over the hedge, the well-loved Dane won't be hard to find—he's right there by your side.

Danes love a cozy place to rest. Disdain's A Dozer, owned by the author, prefers the sofa.

Dogs are pack animals and you are part of the pack! Walhalla's Leibestraum CD, CGC and Siegreich's Amstel V. Nahallac CDX, CGC consider the Miniature Pinscher, Ch. Seigreich's Danksagung V. J-T CD, CGC, TDI and Chris and Harry Bredenkamp part of their pack.

He's easygoing, and you will usually know what to expect from him. He wants to please you, and he will if you handle him gently, socialize him well, and be consistent about your expectations. Be warned—he's stubborn about changing the rules. Let him get away with something once, and he'll expect the same indulgence in the future.

He's very affectionate with the family, and sociable with friends and neighbors. He may, however, be restrained and aloof with strangers. He usually meets new people with a quiet self-confidence, not exactly suspicious but reserving judgement. He's relaxed and calm, but ready to be protective if necessary. This dog is not short on courage, but he seldom gets excited over nothing.

Most Danes are devoted to children, and dependable with them. Still, this is not a dog for the toddler set. He is an excellent companion for older children and teenagers.

This dog is 100% house pet. He needs a close, loving family and a soft, warm bed. He's got spirit and can be playfully rambunctious, but the Dane loves to lounge around the house in comfort much of the time. He'll do just fine raised with other animals, and should have a companion pet—preferably an opposite-sex Dane or other large dog—if the family is usually out all day.

Raise him with love and care; train him with patience and consistency. You'll be proud to have this delightful and reliable companion in the family!

These Dane pups are the picture of good health. They come from Dee Dee Danes, owned by Darthy Davis, of Coal Township, Pennsylvania.

6

FIRST THINGS FIRST

You've decided on a Great Dane. You feel confident that this is the breed for you. You're ready, willing and able to provide a good home. Time to check the pet store or the newspaper and bring the little guy home, right? Wrong! To raise a great dog, you need lots of patience. If you don't have it already, now is the best time to acquire it.

If you choose a puppy on impulse, because it is cute and available now, you are likely to be very sorry later. All puppies are cute and lovable, but that's not enough. Poorly bred dogs may have serious problems. The puppy you are adding to your family should be bred for good health and temperament. Unfortunately, you're not likely to know the difference unless you first learn what you are looking for, where you should go to find it, and what questions you should ask when you get there. You wouldn't plunk down several hundred dollars for a new kitchen stove without knowing whether or not it's electric, has a self-cleaning oven, is white or almond, etc. would you? Shouldn't you be even more careful when buying a living companion to share your home and your life?

With a little extra time and research—and patience—your chances of obtaining your perfect puppy skyrocket. You want to make sure that your new best buddy isn't likely to suffer from inherited diseases and disabilities. You want to know that he isn't likely to be a danger to you or your children. And you want to be spared the heartbreak of giv-

It pays to do your homework. Your dog will share your life for eight or more years. Kevin Zondervan is great friends with future Ch. Mei-Ling's Jordon Ultimo CDX, CGC, TT, owned by his mom, Jill.

ing up or euthanizing the pet you love, simply because an unscrupulous breeder cared only for the money he could make, not for the good health and temperament of the dog he sold to you. This chapter and the remainder of this first section are designed to help you make the right decisions, hopefully culminating in the perfect choice of a healthy, happy companion Dane.

Write a letter to the American Kennel Club (see Appendix C). The AKC is an invaluable resource for potential dog owners. Ask them for a list of Great Dane breeders in your area. Request also the address of the breed club nearest to you, and addresses of any all-breed clubs in your area. You can also contact the national AKC breed club—The Great Dane Club of America—directly for local club information and breeder referrals. Your search for a breeder can begin from these lists, but remember—registration with the AKC does not guarantee an ethical breeder or a quality puppy. The United Kennel Club is another possible resource.

You might want to pick up the latest copies of *Dog Fancy* and *Dog World* magazines at your bookstore or news stand. Both include lists of breeders in various areas of the country. You will also find enjoyable and informative articles about dogs and dog ownership in general. A listing in a magazine does not guarantee quality; again, these are simply potential sources.

There are a number of breed-specific magazines for Dane lovers (See Appendix C). These magazines feature advertisements from many of the country's top kennels, and will give you an opportunity to see photos of quality dogs from across the country. Even if you don't contact any of the specific breeders listed, you'll have a much better idea of what it takes for a Dane to exemplify the breed standard.

Flam'g Oaks You Little Devil is a healthy 12-week-old harlequin owned by Leonard and Janice Jerue, of Dickinson, Texas.

Another possible source, especially if you live in a large urban area, is the classified section of your local newspaper. If you're going this route, however, you can't be too careful. Unfortunately, many of the really good breeders do not choose to advertise in newspapers. It is very likely that the majority listed will be "backyard breeders"—not a reliable source (see Chapter 8). Before responding to any ads, read the remainder of this section so that you are armed with lots of information and the right questions to ask.

Do you feel like this is a lot to go through just to get a pet? Your Dane will be part of your life for probably eight to ten years, longer if you're lucky. That's a long time to live with a dog that frightens you. Think about the money you could spend on vet visits, medications and surgeries for a dog with a debilitating condition. Think about the heartbreak of seeing your beloved companion in constant pain. Think of the disappointment if your dog is physically unable to take those hikes through the woods you've been dreaming about, or to participate in those flyball events that look like such fun? Remember, you're committed to caring for this dog for its lifetime. The patience you show now will help you to do just that, and will more than pay off in the coming months and years.

This lovely fawn puppy grew up to be Ch. Maitau's Talk Show, owned by Patricia Ciampa and Helen Cross, Maitau Danes, Hollis, New Hampshire.

7

WHILE YOU'RE WAITING...

As you read this chapter, your information from the AKC, UKC and/or GDCA should be on it's way. Perhaps you've marked a few magazine and newspaper ads to be called. Chapters eight and nine will help you choose breeders to be interviewed in your search. By now, your puppy is starting to be very real to you. When you find knowledgeable, ethical breeders, things will begin to move much faster. After you choose a breeder, you have only to choose a puppy, which means that now is a great time to do some things that need to be done before Rover—or is it Daisy?—is picked out, paid for and carried home.

First, let's make sure that you and all the members of your household are committed and anxious to take on this responsibility. Just to be absolutely sure (before it's too late) that you want to add a dog to your family, ask yourself the following questions:

1. Is there an adult in your household willing to take primary responsibility for the care of the dog?
2. Is anyone in your family allergic to dogs?
3. Are you sure you have time for playing, grooming, exercising, training, socializing, loving, health care, etc.? And that there is someone willing to do these things?
4. Are the kids in the family old enough to handle such a large dog? Is anyone likely to be afraid of the dog?

It's important to socialize your Dane puppy. Grindstone MVP Wynne Wendy and Grindstone Dolly Sioux, owned by Gay Hughes, of Carmi, Illinois, meet the public.

5. Does everyone want this puppy? Are the expectations of the pup's role in the family clear?

6. Do you have proper facilities for the dog? A soft, quiet place to sleep? A sizable yard?

7. Can you afford quality food and care?

8. Are you willing to put forth extra money and effort to raise, train and care for this dog whenever necessary?

9. Do you realize you may have to deal with barking, accidents on the rug, decimated flower beds and chewed shoes?

10. Are you determined to provide love, affection and quality care for the life of this dog?

If you're still committed, then let's start making preparations! Familiarize yourself with the Breed Standard (Appendix A) and the Breeder's Code of Ethics (Appendix B). Even if you're not looking for a show quality Dane, you should be aware of the guidelines governing breeders and the characteristics they should be working to achieve.

You can begin to buy some basic supplies now. Most things shouldn't wait until you get your puppy—they need to be on hand when she arrives at her new home. You will want to wait on a collar, since it will need to be well-fitted, and food, which will be discussed with the breeder. You should certainly pick up a few safe toys (see Chapter 37). Consider stainless steel food and water bowls. They are indestructible and easy to keep clean. Keep in mind that later on your Dane will need her dishes elevated off the floor. You can purchase dishes with a 19-20" stand now, using the dishes alone until she's tall enough to use the stand. A six foot leash will be usable throughout the dog's life. Leather is especially nice because it is strong, easy to grip and long lasting. Read the crate training information

Kids should be old enough to handle a large dog. Seven-year-old Kyle Zondervan, of San Jose, California, hangs on tight to future Ch. Mei-Ling's Jordon Ultimo CDX, CGC, TT.

in Chapter 17. You can expect to spend quite a bit for a crate, but it will save you money, time and frustration in the months and years to come. Pick up basic grooming tools (see Chapter 19). You'll want to buy a calendar or datebook with room for notations. This will help you to keep track of shots coming due, heartworm preventive to be given, training class schedules and even expenses, if you like.

If you don't already have a trusted vet, choose one now. You'll want someone close to home, if possible. Other pet owners in your neighborhood may be able to give you good referrals. Call the clinic and explain that you'll be getting a puppy very soon. Ask what would be the best time to drop by the facility for a look around. You don't want to be a nuisance or waste their time, but you need to know in advance that they are qualified to care for your pet. Following are some guidelines to use on your visit.

1. Did the vet(s) graduate from an accredited school of veterinary medicine? Is she associated with the American Veterinary Medicine Association? Does she participate in continuing education classes and seminars? Are licenses, diplomas, etc. on view in the clinic or office?
2. Are the clinic hours convenient for you? Do they have emergency facilities on the premises, or work with an emergency clinic nearby?
3. Are the facilities clean? Does it look like a professional medical practice? Is the staff helpful, efficient and professional?
4. Can you ask questions and have them answered in layman's language? Will the Doctor explain her care plan in advance, including any charges? Does she refer to specialists when a problem is beyond her area of expertise? Does she have facilities for x-rays and other diagnostic procedures?
5. Does the Doctor have experience with Great Danes and other giant breeds? Is she familiar with their growth patterns and nutritional needs? Are the

Will your Dane be allowed on the furniture? Dagmar's Bella, owned by Donna Osborn, makes herself comfortable. Bella was bred by Penny and Rick Garcia, Dagmar Danes, Pasadena, Texas.

facilities geared to kennelling and caring for a very large dog?

Once you have your veterinarian lined up, grab your record book and jot down her office and emergency phone numbers, along with the number of the nearest Poison Control Center. Now, let's "puppy proof" your house to cut down on the chances of having to use those numbers.

Pick up and put away anything that Daisy might view as chewable. Danes are taller than other dogs; they quickly grow to reach tabletops, counters, shelves, etc. Keep breakables out of potential reach of a whiplike tail in happy motion. A Dane can wreck a room with her tail alone.

In and around any home, there are numerous everyday items that could be dangerous to your dog: slippery floors and surfaces; certain house and yard plants; chemically treated lawns; rubber bands; disposable razors; anything small enough to swallow; kid's toys; Christmas decorations; any chemical, cleaner or poison; bones and other leftovers; hot pots; sewing and craft supplies; chocolate; alcohol; medications; snakes in tall grass; ants, bees and other insects. An excellent rule of thumb: If it wouldn't be safe for a two year old child, it's not safe for your puppy.

Now is a great time for a little "education session" with the family. Everyone is excited, and talking about the puppy anyway. Read Chapter 11 and decide if a male or female is best for you. You have plenty of time to decide what activities you and your Dane may enjoy when she's older, but if you expect her to shine at obedience, tracking, etc. you should choose from a line of dogs bred for your particular event. Discuss your expectations now. If you're even remotely considering a show dog, read and discuss Chapter 12. Skim through the training information (Chapter 22) and begin checking out puppy kindergarten classes in your area.

Make some preliminary decisions about house rules. It's very confusing for a puppy when the rules are different person-to-person and minute-to-minute. Will the puppy be allowed on the furniture? Where will she eat and sleep? Decide now not to permit the puppy—even once—to do anything you wouldn't feel comfortable allowing her to do when she's fully grown.

Explain to the kids in the family that the puppy has feelings, and is not a toy. Encourage them to share in daily care, and to enjoy games and activities together. Make it clear that Rover is not to be hauled around, screamed at, hit, chased, etc. Remind them that puppies want love and attention just as they do, and should never be teased or tormented. All family members should resolve to be patient and kind. Efforts to win your dog's faith and trust and to be her best friend will be returned in a thousand different ways, including with undying loyalty. And you're going to love those warm, wet puppy kisses!

8

PUPPY MILLS, PET SHOPS AND BACKYARD BREEDERS

Buyer beware! There are some places where you should never buy a dog. Since you are about to go shopping for your new companion, you must recognize these hazards—and steer clear.

Puppy mills are horrible places where innocent animals are forced to live in filth and degradation. Cramped cages, poor food, awful living conditions, no exercise, no healthcare, no toys, no love—they exist only to produce puppies over and over again until their bodies and spirits simply give out. The puppies may or may not be purebred, despite what it says on the registration papers. They may have health and temperament problems—perhaps severe problems. Some don't survive puppyhood in spite of the new owner's best efforts. Why does this sin against man's best friend continue? For money. It's pure greed, plain and simple.

Where are these puppies sold to the unsuspecting public? In a number of places, including pet shops like the one at your local mall. There may be some reputable pet shops out there, but it's probably best to avoid them altogether. Pet supply stores offering pet adoptions, in conjunction with local shelters, are completely different, so please do not confuse the two.

It is difficult to raise and train a dog that is excessively shy and fearful, has phobias or is just plain mean. And it's hard to hear about the heart murmur, hip dysplasia, blindness or whatever affliction that your mill-bred puppy may have. It could also cost a fortune to attempt to care for this dog. The purchase alone costs at least as much as—and possibly more than—you would have paid to a good breeder selling well-bred puppies with health and temperament guarantees!

Why would anyone buy a puppy who may have come from a puppy mill? Lots of reasons. Many people have no idea that this travesty exists. Others don't know where to find a breeder, but they're only ten minutes from the mall. Still others are in a hurry. Maybe they're buying a birthday gift, or they are depressed and want instant gratification. Many of us feel sorry for the puppies sitting in their little cages with their noses pressed against the glass, or simply fall in love when the attendant places that warm, wiggling bundle of fur in our arms. Any puppy can sell itself if you hold it for a few minutes. Why not buy one? The red, white and blue signs all over the store even proclaim "USDA approved." It may seem almost un-American to walk away empty handed, yet walk away you should!

Because they take up too much cage space, you don't often find Great Danes in pet shop windows. But some do carry them, or can order one for you. Before you place your order, there are a few things you should think about. When you buy from a good breeder, you buy a great deal of knowledge and expertise along with your puppy that you just can't get from a pet store. Pet store sales people are just that—sales people. They are not dog experts, capable of assessing the quality and temperament of the dog and providing the information you will need to choose the right dog for you, raise it properly and live with it happily. Your reputable Great Dane breeder has lots of experience in caring for and living with Danes, and is an invaluable resource for you, the puppy buyer.

Beware also of the puppy miller who cuts out the middle man (the pet store) and sells mill-bred Dane pups direct. Respond to their newspaper ad and they may even

It's extremely important to choose a reputable breeder. This 8-week-old is healthy and gorgeous. Walhalla's Liebestraum CD, CGC is owned by Chris and Henry Bredenkamp, Siegreich Danes, in Texas.

offer to bring the litter by your house the same day! They'll arrive promptly with the Dane pups—and perhaps some retriever pups, Doberman pups and Rottweiler/Pit Bull mixes ("Great protection dogs—want to look at them, too?"). They will make every attempt to insure that there's a puppy in that car that will tug at your heart strings—not to mention your purse strings. Keep in mind that good breeders are careful about who purchases their puppies. They want to know that each pup is going to a caring and responsible home. Anyone who is concerned only about your ability to pay for the pup, with no other questions asked, should be suspect. If a red flag begins to wave inside your head, and you think you may be dealing with puppy millers, say "no, No, NO!" Don't give them any reason to continue to subject our sweet, majestic Great Danes to those deplorable living conditions.

It is certainly true that a pup bought from a highly reputable breeder can turn out to have a health or structural problem, or a bad temperament. It is equally true that the pup you buy from the mall or the back of a station wagon may turn out to be beautiful, healthy and sweet. However, it is much more likely to be just the opposite.

Even if you get very, very lucky and your mill-bred puppy is healthy and well-adjusted, you have become one of the reasons why the puppy mills exist, and thrive. If we do not support puppy millers and the retail outlets who sell their dogs, there will be no reason for them to stay in business! Do both yourself and these exploited dogs a favor—adopt your new family member from a reputable breeder or a Dane rescue group!

The next chapter will help you to avoid backyard breeders by telling you the questions to ask, and the answers a reputable breeder is likely to give. But before we

Good breeders take pride in producing mentally and physically sound pups. These five-week-old puppies, born at Alice Haynes' Pappy Jack Danes, in Medford, New York, are almost ready for a new home.

get to that happier task, let's make sure you know enough about this group to avoid them. They may live in the richest or poorest neighborhood. Many of them are just out to make a few bucks, like the puppy millers. They may sell their pups out of the backyard, the formal living room or the back of a pickup in the supermarket parking lot. The worst thing about them is that, when it comes to breeding, they don't know what they're doing—or they know but they don't care.

It is very important, though sometimes difficult, to differentiate between backyard breeders and reputable "hobby" breeders. The professional breeder typically has a large and modern kennel set-up and a great number of dogs. They tend to be very active in conformation showing, and their lives and livelihood may well revolve around breeding quality dogs and finishing championships. The hobby breeder, on the other hand, may have only one or two Danes. They are probably shown in conformation or obedience, and are of reasonably good breeding quality. The hobby breeder is conscientious about choosing the right stud for the right female, providing proper care for dam and pups, and finding quality homes. A good hobby breeder is "professional," yet on a much smaller scale. The backyard breeder, for want of a better term, is not concerned with such things as breeding only within color varieties, carefully matching the dogs to be bred, or performing genetic testing prior to breeding. Those who fall into this category tend to be relatively uninformed people who have an unspayed female and know someone who has an unneutered male. Put the two together and voila! Puppies!!!

Backyard breeders may love their dog dearly—or not. They may take excellent care of her—or not. They may have bred her because she's so sweet that they wanted a puppy just like her, or because she's cost them a fortune and they want some of their money back. The breeding may have been "accidental," or a planned effort to teach the kids about the miracle of birth. But whatever they did, the problem is what they didn't do.

They didn't test for genetic defects before breeding (may not even know what genetic problems are prevalent in Danes). They didn't breed because the bitch is excellent quality, and they found a stud male with the perfect characteristics to produce even better puppies. They didn't work with their local and national breed club, read every available piece of literature about Danes and breeding, train and show Danes, study the standards, pore over pedigrees and do everything humanly possible to insure physical and mental soundness in the pups they produce. They didn't do all these things and more that good breeders do in an effort to better the breed and place quality puppies in excellent homes. Maybe they will sell the pup at a discount price; even so, you'll spend much, much more in the long run. Keep looking—you'll be glad you did.

9

CHOOSING A BREEDER

You don't have your Dane yet, but you've already committed a great deal of time and money to his health and happiness. Now is not the time to run out of patience—you're almost there!

Make a call to the breed club in your area, and to any all-breed clubs about which you've received information. Ask them to recommend Dane breeders, and add any names to your list of possibilities. Ask if there are any shows being held locally. Dog shows are great places to look over good representatives of the breed, and possibly get a few more breeder referrals.

The breeder you choose should be involved in the world of dogs, showing in breed or obedience and preferably active in the breed club. Don't be afraid to ask! He should obviously care a lot about dogs, especially Great Danes. When you call or visit a breeder, expect a willingness to answer all your questions. A breeder who won't be straight with you about the special needs and problems of Great Danes is not ethical. Keep looking.

Discuss hereditary problems in Danes, and how the breeder makes sure these problems are not present in his lines. All good breeders test breeding stock for hip dysplasia, and should be able to show you a certificate from the Orthopedic Foundation for Animals or Penn-Hip stating that the hips of the parents are sound. Most top breeders also check for heart and eye problems, proper thyroid func-

Good health and temperament are important and these eight-week-old fawn pups have both. Brees' Oprah's On (now championship pointed) and Brees' Peaches are owned by Debbie Cole, Bree Danes, of Garland, Texas.

tion, and autoimmune diseases. OFA now has registries for thyroid diseases and congenital heart disease, as well as hips and elbows. Don't accept the breeder's word—ask to see the paperwork. Proof of certification from the Orthopedic Foundation for Animals and the Canine Eye Registry Foundation (CERF) can now be found on AKC registration certificates.

Don't be shy about questioning a breeder's experience and integrity. How many breeds does he raise? If it's more than two, be wary. How many litters does he breed every year? You want someone who breeds for quality, not quantity. Does he adhere to the Breeder's Code of Ethics? For what characteristics does he typically breed? He may talk about movement and structure, but if it's not apparent that good health and temperament are of primary importance, move on.

Does the breeder seem to have a good relationship with his dogs? Do they approach him with confidence, and obey him happily? Is he affectionate with the dogs? Do both the dogs and the premises look clean?

Ask why this particular breeding took place. The breeder should be able to explain the characteristics of the sire that were expected to complement those of the dam, and whether or not he feels this was accomplished. The aim should be to use only top quality breeding stock, and to produce puppies that are even better than the parents.

Ask to see the dam. She may not be at her best while nursing pups, but she should be basically healthy and happy. Pay attention to her looks, personality and temperament. Would you like to have a dog very much like her? If not, you probably don't want one of her pups. The sire may or may not be available, but the breeder should have pictures or a videotape to show you, along with a copy of the pedigree. How old are the dam and sire? Each should be in their prime, but no less than two years of age. It's a big

You should observe the relationship between the breeder and his dogs. Sandy Hann clearly gets along well with Ch. Von Shrado's I'm A Knock Out. (Von Shrado Danes, Pikeville, North Carolina)

plus if either or both have obedience or other titles to their credit, a breed championship or points toward championship status.

How old will the pups be before the breeder will let them go? They should be at least eight weeks, and have been given their first puppy shots. Will a veterinarian check them over before they go to new homes? Are they being socialized? If the pups are spending eight weeks or more in a kennel with little human contact, try another breeder.

What about guarantees? Will the breeder guarantee that the pup has no contagious diseases at the time of sale, and for a reasonable period thereafter? Are there at least a few days in which you may return the pup for any reason? Is there a guarantee against severe hereditary problems for at least one year? Does the breeder also guarantee temperament? Are all the details, including return or replacement policies, spelled out in writing?

Is the breeder willing to give advice on housebreaking, training, grooming, feeding? Are his dogs on premium food, and will a small supply go home with the pup? Will you receive the registration slip and a copy of the pedigree when you pick up your puppy? Can you still call the breeder with questions next month? Next year?

Ask to review any contracts you will be expected to sign when you purchase a pup. The contract should include a full description of the dog being sold, terms of payment, specific guarantees, return and refund policies, spay and neuter agreements, and a list of rights, if any, being retained by the breeder. The contract may state that a pet quality puppy is being sold with limited registration. This means that the particular puppy is not of show or breeding quality. While the puppy himself is AKC registered, any progeny he has in the future will not be eligible for registration. This is a sign of a breeder who wants to protect the breed and insure that only the finest quality Danes are bred. Your Dane with limited registration will still be eligible to compete in activities such as flyball, tracking, etc., and can earn

It's a plus if you can meet the sire. Eight-week-old Siegreich's Amstel V. Nahallac CDX, CGC hangs out with her pop, Walhalla's Liebestraum CD, CGC at the home of Chris and Henry Bredenkamp, Siegreich Danes, Burleson, Texas.

titles in these activities. Make sure you understand each item of the contract before you agree to buy.

Remember that the best way to get answers is to ask questions, and don't hesitate to ask for references! Expect to answer as many questions as you ask. The reputable breeder cares what happens to his puppies, and will only place them in good homes. He'll want to make sure that you have both the money and the facilities to provide for this dog, that you know what to expect, and that the puppy will have a stable, loving home. The breeder will be impressed and reassured by the pertinent questions you ask, and by your efforts to find just the right companion for you and your family.

15 POTENTIAL HEALTH CONCERNS IN DANES

It's best to discuss these conditions with breeders before choosing your Dane pup.

Bloat—Serious emergency in which stomach fills up with air; may cause stomach to twist; puts extreme pressure on internal organs. (See Chapter 31)

Bone tumors—Not a common problem, but occurs in older Danes, usually on the leg. Lameness and swelling are typical symptoms. Can cause amputation or death.

Calluses—Danes often get calluses, or wrinkled, thickened skin areas, from lying on concrete or other hard surfaces. They are typically found at pressure points like the elbow. They don't look very good, and they can become sore and infected. Calluses can be softened somewhat with petroleum jelly, but a thick, soft bed to sleep on will prevent them from ever occuring.

Cardiac problems—Congenital heart disease is genetic. Symptoms are usually noted in the puppy. Cardiomyopathy is acquired in adulthood, and may be genetic or caused by a viral infection. Many dogs with cardiomyopathy are also hypothyroid. Causes heart muscle to thicken and stiffen or conversely become thin and flabby. Eventually leads to congestive heart failure. Seen most often in male Danes under five years of age.

Cataracts—Clouding of the eye lens. Often seen in diabetic dogs. Can lead to blindness. Surgery is difficult and not always an option.

Degenerative myelopathy—Neurological problem causing weakness in the rear limbs and eventually paralysis. Not painful but progressive. The cause is not known.

Epilepsy—Neurological problem characterized by seizures. Can be caused by infections, trauma, strokes or can be of unknown cause. Can bring about temporary changes in behavior, gait or vision. Can be difficult to treat.

Hip dysplasia—Faulty development of the hip joint characterized by lameness and pain in hips and hind legs. Degenerative arthritis develops as the hip wears down. Primarily genetic, but affected by environmental factors.

Hypertrophic osteodystrophy—Bone disease affecting young Danes. Pain and fever must be treated, but most dogs recover on their own. Can also cause depression and appetite loss. In severe cases, bones can be permanently deformed. Improper nutritional balance is one possible cause, but many things are thought to trigger HOD or HOD-like symptoms.

66

Hypothyroidism—Endocrine disorder most often seen in young or middle aged Danes. Symptoms usually included sleepiness and lethargy, fatigue, and lack of mental sharpness. Weight changes may or may not be seen. Skin may become scaly or darkly pigmented. Coat is often dry. A great deal of hair loss may occur. Daily medication is necessary, but life span should not be affected with treatment.

Osteochondritis dessicans—Lameness in one or both shoulders or stifles. Can be very painful. A section of cartilage and bone dies, leaving a flap of tissue that irritates the joint. Often requires surgery.

Panosteitis—Inflammatory bone disease seen in immature Danes. Pain is in the long bones of the leg rather than the joints. Lameness may shift from leg to leg. May be caused from excessive protein or calcium in growing periods. Usually self-limiting, but may continue for months. Treatment is geared at relieving pain.

Tail injuries—The Dane has a very strong, whiplike tail. When that tail is wagged fiercely against a solid object such as a floor or wall, splitting sometimes occurs. The tail can bleed profusely and is often difficult to heal. Some Danes develop such severe bruising and even infection that the tail tip must be amputated. A shock cushioning collar can be made of two pieces of sponge rubber held together with rubber cement. Some breeders recommend nasal spray to shrink the blood vessels in the tail tip and promote quicker healing.

Von Willebrands disease—Genetic disorder characterized by profuse bleeding in puppies when teething, when ears are cropped, or when there is trauma such as to the tail. Adults may also have abnormal bleeding. Disease is incurable, but supportive treatment is given.

Wobbler syndrome—Dane puppies who are wobblers have faulty growth of the cervical vertebrae, causing a malformation which pinches the spinal cord and keeps it from functioning properly. Wobblers are unsteady and possibly stiff, may drag their feet or even be unable to stand and walk. Reduced protein and rest can help some wobbler pups through their neurological problems, but others suffer nerve damage and even paralysis.

Other problems seen in Danes include entropion and ectropion (eyelid disorders), bad bites and flat feet, elbow dysplasia, monorchidism and cryptorchidism (undescended testicles), urinary stones, knee problems, megaesophagus (congenital disorder of the esophageal tube), and nasty or unreliable temperaments.

Siegreich's Von Leben UD, TDI has the traditional cropped ear. Owned by Chris and Henry Bredenkamp, Siegreich Danes, Burleson, Texas.

10

THE EAR CROPPING CONTROVERSY

Ear cropping is a hot topic in the dog fancy these days. The English have banned this cosmetic surgery, and many Americans would like to see this country follow suit. Most Great Dane breeders vehemently disagree. For as long as cropping is legal in the country—which may not be very long—the majority of Danes will continue to have altered ears. Decide for yourself.

The Argument For: "In order to achieve the 'Dane look' and to show off the shape of the head, you must crop the ears. Besides, the dogs are less likely to have ear infections and may even hear better. Cropping is traditional in the breed; it was done in the days when Danes fought boars and couldn't afford to have hanging ears for the boars to grab. It still gives them the alert appearance of a working dog, which is as it should be. Cropping adds an additional expense that puppy mills don't wish to take on; therefore Danes as a breed aren't as victimized as they will be if cropping is banned. Take away the crop and you take away much of the dignity and elegant appearance of the Great Dane. Besides, it would take years of selective breeding to produce a decent looking natural ear."

If you decide to crop: It's very possible that the ears may have been done before you even see the puppy. Cropping should be done between seven and ten weeks of age. The pup must be in excellent health and physical condition. The surgery is done under general anesthesia, and

The beautiful Ch. Maitau's Talk Show has a long, elegant ear crop. This lovely bitch is owned by Patricia Ciampa and Helen Cross, Maitau Great Danes, Hollis, New Hampshire.

should only be performed by a licensed veterinarian. Do not allow anyone else to perform surgery on your dog. Make sure the vet is familiar with the Dane crop. The crop does not look exactly like that of other cropped breeds. Follow after-care instructions to the letter. After the ears are cut for correct size and shape, they must be braced and taped erect so that the cartilage will grow upright. Extreme care must be taken to promote healing and prevent infection.

The Argument Against: "Why would you inflict pain on a puppy for purely cosmetic reasons? The surgery is traumatic, and causes suffering. The breed standard for Great Danes accepts natural ears in the show ring. There are even natural champions now. If more people would give up this barbaric practice, ear cropping would soon be *passe.*

And why would you even consider cropping a companion dog that will never compete in the breed ring? You spend weeks or even months afterward taping the ears. It's an ordeal for you and the puppy, and the ears still may not stand. The anesthesia can be dangerous, and infection could set in after the surgery. Will your dog be a better companion because his ears stand? Of course not! Natural ears are beauti-

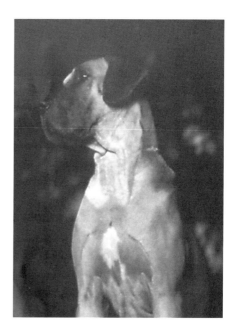

Natural-eared dogs can and do win in the show ring. This is Ch. Mei-Ling's Bogart Rara Avis, owned by Shelley Hayse.

ful. They give the Dane a softer look that is both appealing and in keeping with the temperament of the breed. Besides, Danes have not been used for boar fighting for many years! Stop the mutilation!"

If you believe ears should be natural: Tell breeders that you're looking for an uncropped puppy. If the pup is to be a companion only, you may get little argument. If you're going to show, it will be harder to find a breeder who

Newly cropped ears don't always stand.

will sell to you, but it's not impossible. Danes with natural ears are being bought, sold and shown. Buy the best specimen possible to help counteract the prejudice of some judges against natural ears. Take pride in your dog and remember—the world is turning your way. Twenty-first century Danes will most likely be shown without alteration.

Newly cropped ears must be braced and taped, like those of Magic's Stairway to Heaven, owned by Tom and Kathy Hinson and bred by Linda Altomare, Magic Manor Danes, Hubbard, Ohio.

11

MALE OR FEMALE?

Males are larger yes, but any Dane is a big dog. The males are awesome and masculine; the bitches decidedly feminine and graceful.

A bitch may be a better pet for a novice owner. Many Dane fanciers feel that a female can be a little easier to housebreak and train, and that she is naturally more affectionate and companionable. The bitch may be the best choice if you'd like to get into competitive obedience.

On the down side, a female tends to have more mood swings than the male. If she's not in the mood to be corrected, she may sulk or ignore you all day long. She also has heat periods that can be messy and can disrupt your life entirely. Many unspayed females urine mark their territory, much like a male dog. If she's not a show dog, have her spayed early to prevent her from coming in season (See Chapter 32).

A male may be more active and playful, and will no doubt be protective of his family and property. He's also typically stable in temperament, which may mean he's sweet all the time, or dominant all the time. Still, you pretty much know what to expect. Many male Danes are quite full of themselves, which can be fun if you like an energetic, upbeat dog. It can also be wearing if you'd prefer a calmer, more laid-back pet.

His territorial attitude makes him more likely to mark his surroundings with urine, so he may be difficult

Rolls is a truly masculine male. He's formally known as Am. & Can. Ch. & Can. O.T. Ch. Danehaven's Rolling Thunder UDT, Can. UDTDX, WDX, HC, U-CDX, TDI owned by Marta Brock.

to housebreak. He may also be more destructive. Male Danes tend to be very good at pretending you're not talking to them when you give a command to get off the furniture or out of the garbage. Some are so good at playing deaf and dumb that owners refer to them as "brain dead" (affectionately, of course). The truth is, they are smart enough to know just how far they can push, and gutsy enough to try to get by with just a little bit more than they did last time. Some males, if not properly trained, attempt to challenge and dominate their owners regularly. Some will accept the adults in the house as "alpha," but try to dominate the children in the family. This can be a scary situation for a child, and is potentially dangerous.

If your dog is not a show specimen, early neutering will calm him down and help to avoid excessive dominance and behavior problems. The neutered male will still want to lift his leg on every tree, so walks are a little more complicated than with a female. His urine may also kill off your backyard bushes and shrubs. If you have prize roses, either make sure they are separate from your Dane's yard area, or get a female.

Keep in mind that not all of these generalities will apply to a specific dog. Some males are excellent obedience prospects, and would never dream of ignoring you or trying your patience. Some females are hard to housebreak and train, and pushy enough to remind you of just why the word "bitch" is often used in a less than flattering manner! In any case, proper management makes all the difference. If your Dane will be a second dog in the family, choose the opposite sex from your first dog for best results. Either sex can be a wonderful pet with the right care and training.

Females are feminine and graceful. This is Ch. Sheron's Kahlua N Cream owned by Beverly Hauer and Sherry Acena, Hauerdane, Alpine, California.

Showing dogs can be rewarding. 16 month old Pappy Jack Justin Time Again, owned by Alice Haynes, has nine points. (Ashbey photo)

Owner handlers can and do win in the breed ring. Alice Haynes pilots Papy Jack Sweet Nothing to Best of Winners. She has eight points.

12

DO YOU WANT A SHOW DOG?

What is the difference between show quality and pet quality? Often very little. As a matter of fact, the average person usually cannot tell the difference. The conformation of the show dog adheres very closely to that required by the breed standard. When viewing several puppies in a litter, one may stand out as being more handsome than all the rest. Yet this same puppy may be pet quality, and his siblings show quality, simply because he has a faulty bite that would hurt his chances in the show ring. "Pet quality" may mean that the dog has too many white hairs, or that the ears are a little too long and "houndish." Most show Danes are also companions, and most pet Danes are elegant, attractive dogs.

What's all this fuss about dog shows, anyway? Isn't it simply a matter of personal preference which dog looks the best? The personal preference of the judge does enter into it, because he or she must be the one to interpret the breed standard and decide which dog entered in a particular show is its' best representative. The purpose of conformation is to determine the dogs that are suitable for breeding, with the aim being always to better the breed by using only the finest specimens to produce future generations.

The breed standard is the definitive guideline upon which the judge makes his or her determination. While it may seem that the dogs in the ring are competing against each other, they are really competing against a mental image in the judge's mind of a perfect Great Dane, as described by the breed standard. The judge decides which dog comes closest to that standard of perfection, judging each one on physical structure, condition, gait and temperament. Of all the Danes competing in a single show, only the Winners Dog and Winners Bitch receive points toward their championships. Those who have earned the title of "Champion" have proven their worth under several judges and have received at least 15 points. Conformation will be covered in greater detail in Chapter 33.

If you are interested in showing in breed, you need to find a dog that comes very close to the standard. While no one can say positively that a young puppy will turn out to be show quality, experienced breeders of show dogs have the knowledge and the instincts to make an educated guess. Keep in mind that the biggest is not necessarily the best. The next chapter will give you guidelines for choosing a show prospect puppy. Study the breed standard until you know it backward and forward. Attend shows, and study the competitors until you can see for yourself how the standard applies and what really makes a winner.

Campaigning a dog in breed is not easy and it's not cheap. There is tremendous competition in Danes, and most are handled by professionals who know just how to show off their best attributes. But if you go into it with the spirit of fun and a willingness to learn, sooner or later you'll be an old pro yourself. Everyone has to start somewhere.

Just please remember that the dog you choose is your dog, whether or not he wins in the ring. If the ribbons don't come because you're a poor handler, your dog will continue to love you. If you don't win because of a fault in your dog's conformation, he can and will continue to fulfill the main purpose of every Dane—to be your best friend.

13

CHOOSING YOUR DOG

You've narrowed your search to one or two quality breeders, and from their litters you will choose your special puppy. Choose carefully, because every dog is an individual. You want the one that best fits your lifestyle.

Be very honest with the breeder. Don't swear you want a partner for jogging and frisbee if you really want a Dane who prefers to curl up on the couch and watch Scooby Doo reruns with you. Beyond your basic choices of sex and color, you need to tell the breeder all about your family and your plans for this dog. She can help you to make a proper choice.

The first thing you should look for is a healthy pup. Eyes should be clear and bright, ears clean and dry. The puppy should breathe easily with no runny nose, no coughing or sneezing. There should be no unpleasant odor and no signs of parasites or diarrhea. The puppy should be alert and friendly. Find out as much as you can about the parents; many traits of the dam and sire are likely to show up in the pups. Then watch how the littermates behave with each other to help you determine how a certain puppy is likely to behave with you. Is she pushy, nipping and barking at the other pups? She'll probably be a loud, pushy adult. Does she whine and cry when the other pups play rough with her? She may be just as shy and fearful with you. Many Dane breeders routinely temperament test their puppies, and can tell you a great deal about an individual

These puppies look alike now, but each will grow into a unique individual. Litter owned by Pappy Jack Danes, Alice Haynes, Medford, New York.

pup's personality and temperament. If not, the following guidelines will help you to determine whether or not a specific pup is right for you.

You want a puppy that is interested in you. If you squat down and clap your hands, what does she do? If she's totally uninterested now, she'll probably be an unresponsive adult. If she's frightened now, you may very well be dealing with her fears and timidity throughout her life. Focus your attention on the ones who focus attention on you, and come quickly to see what you're doing.

Sit down with the puppies and watch their reactions. You don't want the one who ignores you and wanders away, or backs away in fear. Remove one puppy from the group and offer petting and attention. When you walk away, will the puppy follow you if you call and encourage him to do so?

Look for a puppy who is curious and confident. This little guy is owned by Beverly Hauer, Hauerdane, Alpine, CA.

Look for a puppy demonstrating interest and confidence, one who is alert and responsive.

Pick up a puppy and cradle it in your arms as you would a baby. If she panics until you release her, don't choose this one. If she struggles for a few seconds, then relaxes, okay. Even better if she's relaxed and comfortable from the beginning.

Drop your key ring near the pups. It's fine if a puppy is not at all bothered by the noise—provided you're sure she can hear—but you can expect most to be startled momentarily.

The older the pup, the more sure you can be of show quality. G'Dieter's Chance Encounter has 7 points toward his championship, including a major, at only 8 months. Owned by Nancy and Gary Gale, of Jupiter, Florida.

The question is, does she run in fear or just startle, then come over to check out the keys? It can be hard to deal with a 150 pound dog that trembles at the sound of passing cars or runs from the vacuum.

Pick up the puppy and squeeze lightly between the toes. She may show discomfort and pull back her paw, but should not yelp loudly or try to bite. She should also be willing to forgive and be friends when you let go. Pups that show a very low tolerance of pain are likely to resist handling during grooming, vet visits, etc.

81

Will the puppy's temperament correspond with that of your family? If she's pushy and aggressive, everyone in the household must be dominant enough to control her. If she's quiet and somewhat shy, you don't want to toss her into a family with three boisterous kids and a whirlwind of activity.

If you're looking for show quality, you will have to rely even more on the integrity and knowledge of the breeder. Keep in mind that many top breeders will not sell their best show prospects to someone who does not have a show background. You will have to convince the breeder that your interest is sincere, and that you have the time and money to campaign the dog. Look for a balanced puppy as close as possible to the breed standard. You want overall structure and soundness, good size, substance and muscle tone. A good show dog must have the proper attitude— that of a show off! She should enjoy looking good and commanding the spotlight, and that enjoyment and "look at me" attitude should be overt and obvious. The older the pup, the more sure you can be of quality. Of course, you could also consider an adult who has been trained for the breed ring and has started her show career.

After reading the previous chapters and talking with breeders, are you concerned that a puppy with its' need for constant care and attention may be too much for you right now? Talk to a breeder or club representative about adopting an adult, perhaps a dog that turned out not to be right for show or breeding, or even a rescue Dane. With the adult, it's easier to see what you're getting. You won't be surprised later at size, looks or temperament. Have each family member spend time with the dog before deciding to adopt, and learn everything you can about her history, training and behavior. It may take patience to fit an adult with set behavior patterns into the family, but it can often be easier than raising a puppy. Dane rescue will be discussed in the next chapter.

14

THE RESCUE DANE

A rescue dog is one that didn't make it in her last home, for whatever reason. A Dane may have become lost, and efforts to reunite her with her owner were unsuccessful. The owner may have died or become too ill to care for the dog, or the dog may be just another victim in a messy divorce. Sometimes a dog has health or temperament problems that the owner chooses not to tackle, whether due to lack of time, money or interest. At least part of the time, these problems are easily treatable.

More often that not, Danes are given up due to basic "doggie" behavior problems, such as jumping on people, barking or chewing excessively or being uncontrollable on lead. These types of behavior problems are typically the fault of an owner who did not provide proper attention and training. Such problems can almost always be rectified, but it will no doubt take work and patience on the part of a new owner to retrain an older puppy or adult dog.

Those breeders and fanciers who do Great Dane rescue usually do an excellent job of evaluating the dog's health and temperament, and determining her suitability for a new home and family. Many breeders are available to take back one of their dogs if the owner must give the dog up. Unfortunately, not all breeders are so ethical, so caring Dane breeders and clubs do their best to pick up the slack created by careless breeders who feel no responsibility toward the puppies they breed.

Rescue groups are not all the same. One group may

be in a different state of organization and development than another, and this fact may be reflected in the services they do or do not provide. Usually, the longer a group has been participating in rescue, the more volunteers and money they have accumulated to further their efforts. One group may spay or neuter all dogs prior to adoption; another may have you sign a contract agreeing to have the dog altered within a reasonable length of time. One group may house Danes in foster homes or kennels throughout a geographical area; another may only provide a matching service, helping interested adopters to locate available Danes in shelters or homes where the owner wishes to give up the dog. The fee typically reflects the services provided. You can expect to pay more for a Dane that has been health checked, immunized, wormed, neutered, etc. than for one who has only received shots and daily food.

Before you adopt from a rescue group, ask to read the contract you will be expected to sign. Most are very reasonable, but you want to make sure that you can live in accordance with a particular contract. For instance, if the contract requires a fenced yard and you plan to move to an apartment in six months, will the rescue group remove the dog from your home? If the group requires that you attend a basic obedience course given by them, but you are unavailable every Monday night and decide to train your Dane elsewhere, are you in violation of the contract? For the sake of the dog you are adopting, make sure all agreements are clear. Both you and the rescue group should be working to assure that the Dane you are adopting will not lose out on another home after bonding with your family.

Make an effort to get to know everything you can about your prospective Dane. Ask lots of questions that would relate to your lifestyle and home situation. Has she lived with cats? Does he like other dogs? Is he protective of his food? Is she crate trained? Ask also about health care. Did the previous owner give heartworm preventive regularly? Has the dog been wormed by the rescue group? Are vaccinations current? The rescue group may or may not

It is the aim of rescue programs to place dogs in lifelong loving homes. A young Disdain's A Dozer was saved from an abusive situation. Patience and love have been rewarded by loyalty and affection. Dozer adores Michael and author Mary McCracken, of Houston.

know about the home the dog came from, or the care that was provided. They will, however, be able to tell you about their experiences with the dog, the little behavior traits they've noticed, and the care they've given.

Be very open with rescuers about your personality, your family and your home. The rescue organization should do temperament testing on each dog, or at least careful observation over a period of time. The more they know about both you and the dog, the better they can match the right dog with your lifestyle. Again, the Dane in question has already lost one home. The aim should be to place the dog in a secure, loving, responsible home for the rest of his life. The rescue group should provide you with educational materials to help you understand and care for the dog, and should be available by telephone to answer your questions.

Make sure everyone in your family wants this particular dog. Run through the list of commitment questions in Chapter seven to be sure. Have each person spend one-on-one time with the dog PRIOR to the adoption. Maybe you could take him to a nearby park and just hang out with him for a while. Make sure he's really YOUR dog. If anyone in the family will want to "take him back" for chewing on a shoe or muddying the carpet, face the fact that the commitment just isn't there and don't adopt the dog.

You must have patience to adopt a rescue dog. This Dane you've added to your life may have had some very rough times. She may be easily frightened and have trouble placing trust in you. She may be poorly trained, and may do a number of things that displease you before you are able to bond with her and teach her the rules of the house. She may be nervous, and may show her frustrations by chewing or house soiling. Still, your chances are very good that the efforts you make will pay off and she will quickly blossom into the Dane you were hoping for. Typically, once a rescue dog realizes that you're really hers, that you love her and that she is safe and secure, she will work diligently to please you. Her world will revolve around you, her savior. This can definitely be one of the most rewarding ways to obtain a family companion, but you must have patience to establish trust and create a bond with the dog. Provide your rescue Dane with love and security and you could end up with the most loyal pet of all.

Whether or not you adopt a rescue Dane, you can be part of the solution in the serious pet overpopulation problem. Consider helping the rescue effort. Perhaps you could provide a temporary foster home for a Dane, participate in a fund raising event, or include Dane rescue on your personal list of charities to support.

Maybe you could write or type an occasional newsletter article, help once a month to bathe dogs not yet adopted, or take phone calls from potential adopters now and then. You can tell friends and coworkers who are considering adding a dog to their family that rescue dogs of every breed are out there awaiting new homes. And for the sake of your Dane's health and your peace of mind, as well as pet overpopulation, SPAY OR NEUTER YOUR COMPANION GREAT DANE!

15

BEFORE YOU BRING PUPPY HOME

Skim through Chapter seven again. Do you have a vet chosen for the little guy? Walk through your home once more and make sure it's safe for your new puppy or adult Dane. Did you decide on the basic rules of behavior? Are there dishes, toys and other supplies waiting at home, including a crate? If there's anything missing, pick it up before you take Rover home. Ask the breeder or rescue worker to help you measure him for a proper fitting collar, and pick up a bag of the food the breeder or rescue organization suggests.

Make sure you have a phone number to contact the breeder or rescue personnel when you have questions. Make an appointment with the vet to check out your Great Dane within 48 hours of taking him home.

Even if it means leaving your new friend behind for a few more days, be sure that you are ready and that Rover's new home is prepared and properly stocked. The best time to take him home is in the morning, preferably at the beginning of a vacation or long weekend. He should be comfortable with his new home and family before he's left alone. If you're bringing him home tonight and everyone will be rushing off to work and school in the morning, how will he ever feel secure, or become housebroken and trained? Make sure you are totally prepared for this responsibility before you put that puppy or dog into your car and he becomes a member of the family—til death do us part, remember?

Black Zeus of T's Mist and Disdain's A Dozer, owned by the author, sport "everyday" nylon collars.

Dagmar's Morgon, owned by Penny and Rick Garcia, wears a training collar.

Dagmar's Sohni is spiffy in rolled leather. Owned by Dagmar Danes, Pasadena, Texas.

Maitau girls in show leads. Seven-year-old Maitau's Village Gossip, 12-year-old Ch. Maitau's Conversation Piece and 10-year-old Ch. Maitau's Tattletale are owned by Patricia Ciampa and Helen Cross.

CHOOSING COLLARS FOR YOUR DANE

You will need a buckle collar for everyday use. The buckle collar should be the only collar used on your very young puppy. The collar should fit high on the neck and should be loose enough for you to slip in two fingers but tight enough not to slip over the head. To fit a buckle collar, use a tape measure to obtain the circumference of the neck, and add one to two inches. A wider collar is more protective of the throat because it lessens pressure on the esophagus. You have lots of choices in buckle collars. Leather is long lasting and a good choice as a permanent collar once your Dane reaches adulthood. Rolled leather is especially comfortable and causes less breakage of the coat. Nylon collars come in a wide variety of colors and patterns, including special collars for holidays. Nylon is reasonably priced and is washable. You can choose the "old-fashioned" metal hole-and-ladder closure, or the newer "quick-release" type. Many are adjustable—great for your adolescent Dane. If your dog has an allergic reaction to his collar, consider cotton web.

A training collar will be needed for your adolescent-to-adult Dane. Chain slip collars are designed to "pop and release" for corrections during training. Collars with wider links are preferable. Add three inches to the neck measurement for proper fit. It is very important that training collars be used properly. Ask your breeder or obedience trainer for a demonstration. Training collars should be used only in training situations where the dog is supervised. Many dogs have been injured or killed when a slip collar became entangled and strangled the dog.

The buckle and training collars will be relied upon for the life of your Dane. However, there are a number of other collars for special situations. Prong collars should only be used by highly experienced trainers, if at all. Show leads are used in the conformation ring, and are a one-piece leash and thin collar which is designed to give maximum control. Headcollars fit around the muzzle and head, and are considered a humane alternative to a chain slip collar. For Danes that pull, there are collar/halter combinations that allow control without hurting the dog. Appendix C lists sources for collars and other training equipment.

SECTION II
BRINGING UP BABY

Your puppy will have to make the transition from living with his littermates to living in your home. These lovely blue pups were bred by Linda Altomare, Magic Manor Danes, Hubbard, Ohio.

At first the puppy may be lonely. This nine-week-old brindle is Maitau's Taylor Made Alano, owned by Patricia Ciampa and Helen Cross, Maitau Danes, Hollis, New Hampshire.

16

IN THE BEGINNING...

Leaving his mom and littermates is traumatic for your puppy. It's up to you to make the transition as easy as possible. Whether you realize it or not, you begin training your Dane when he walks through your door. Within a day or two, he'll know if you are a trustworthy, patient, in-charge type of person to be respected and loved, or a loud, impatient, inconsistent person to be ignored or feared.

Stay calm. It's okay to pet and love little Rover, but give him a chance to explore and learn about his new home—with supervision, of course. Pay close attention to his natural routine. Does he need a nap after a 20-minute play session? Does he relieve himself right after he eats, or does he wait half an hour? The more you know about the natural inclinations of this puppy, the easier it will be to teach him all the things he needs to know. This time of observation and getting to know one another is just as important if you have adopted an adult or rescue Dane.

During the first few days in his new home, he needs supervision virtually all the time. Keep in mind that your baby Dane will already be larger than many adult dogs, and therefore capable of bigger messes and more destruction. If you must go out for an hour or so, put the pup in his crate with a safe toy and blanket, and soft noise from the radio or TV in the background. Make sure he's had ample opportunity to relieve himself before you crate him.

Ten-week-old Diamond's Leather and Lace CGC may need a nap after playing with Kevin Zondervan. "Tanner" is owned by Jill Zondervan and Shelley Hayse, San Jose, California.

You'll probably want to place his crate near your bed for at least the first several nights. If he cries and won't settle down, a stuffed toy or hot water bottle may help, or try a ticking clock just outside the crate. Don't let him in your bed now unless he'll be allowed to sleep with you all the time, even when he's a 150 pound adult! Just try to provide an adequate substitute for the warmth of his brothers and sisters until he gets used to his new surroundings.

Remember that a dog is a creature of habit. The quicker he learns his daily routine, the quicker he will relax and begin to fit into the household. He needs to know how you expect him to behave, and when he can expect food, walks, playtime and an opportunity to relieve himself. Your puppy, or adult Dane, is completely dependent on you for his most basic needs. You must calmly teach him the rules, and the sooner, the better.

He needs a name, and not just the formal name on his registration papers. He needs a simple name that you will use to call him every day. One or two syllables with strong vowel sounds is best. Pick a name that will convey a happy, positive image; you may think "Killer" is cute but it may make neighbors and veterinarians fearful and resentful of your wonderful dog. To have everyone afraid of this big guy could make you unwelcome everywhere! Make sure his name won't be easily confused with commands or with the names of other animals or people in the household. Calling Bo, and telling Bo "no" could get pretty confusing, as could two dogs named Dude and Duke, or a dog named Sammy who belongs to Tammy.

Your Dane is completely dependent on you. These Pappy Jack pups—one 7 months, the other 5 weeks—know they can count on Mom, Alice Haynes, for love and care.

As soon as you've chosen a name, put an identification tag on his collar with his name, address and phone number. Plan to take photos early and frequently. Not only will you enjoy reminiscing over his baby pictures some day, you will also have current photos in case he's ever lost. There are other ways to protect your Dane from being lost or stolen. Almost all shelters, rescue organizations and research labs who could come into possession of a lost dog know to look for a tattoo. Tattoos

Dagmar's Sundance shows off her identification tag. Sundance is owned by Penny and Rick Garcia, Dagmar Danes, Pasadena, Texas.

are typically placed on the inside of the thigh where they don't affect the good looks of your dog, can be applied painlessly, and can't be lost or removed the way a collar and tag can. It is illegal for a research facility to keep or use a tatooed animal. The tatoo can be registered with one or more organizations that will contact you if your Dane is reported found. You can also microchip your Dane, which will most likely be the 21st century protection of choice. Unfortunately, the technology is not sufficiently advanced to make the microchip invaluable as yet. Put up a couple of "Beware of Dog" signs around your property, and place "Pet Alert" stickers in windows to alert rescue personnel to the presence of a dog in case of emergency.

Start right now to treat your Dane as the family member he needs to be. Take him along when you drop the kids at school. Toss a ball for him to chase when you're relaxing on the patio in the evenings. He'll learn more just being with you and sharing your life than he ever could with harsh training and punishment. Be consistent about the rules, but relax—raising and training your Great Dane can be fun!

17

HOUSEBREAKING AND CRATE TRAINING

Both housebreaking and crate training should begin immediately. Using the crate will certainly make housebreaking easier, but it's very important to use the crate properly, as there is much potential for misuse.

Your puppy's crate is a bed, a den, and a safe haven. It is not a punishment or a jail. Why do you put a baby in a playpen? So that the baby can play or rest safely in its own place while you are busy. You crate a puppy for the same reasons.

The crate should be large enough for Daisy to lie down, stand, stretch and turn around. If your crate is designed for an adult Dane, partition part of it off until she grows into it.

Introduce the crate slowly. Toss in a treat and let her go in after it when she's ready. Leave the door open at first. Serve dinner in the crate, again letting her enter and exit when she's ready. Once she's comfortable going in and out, toss in a treat and shut the door behind her. Start with only a minute or two of crate time. If she whines when you close the door, firmly say "No, Quiet" and wait to open the door. As soon as she's quiet, let her out. You want her to associate good behavior with getting what she wants. If you open the door when she whines and cries, she'll learn very quickly that whining gets results. Gradually increase the time until she learns that the crate is a safe, quiet place to rest. Use the crate for naps and to confine her if you must leave for a while. Always leave a safe toy or two in the crate. If you have to leave for several hours, place both Daisy and the crate in a safe, easy to clean area like the kitchen and leave the crate open.

Each time she goes to enter her crate, say "Daisy, crate." Before you know it, she'll enter her crate on command. Once she's inside, say "Good girl, Daisy, crate!" NEVER send your dog to her crate for punishment. The crate is her own special place and should be associated with comfort, quiet and security, never punishment. It's her refuge when she's tired or stressed, and she'll willingly use it for the rest of her life if she's properly trained as a pup.

The crate can be used in your bedroom at night, but if you're going to crate Daisy for an hour while you clean the kitchen, place her nearby where she can safely observe your activity. The crate can quicken the housebreaking process, prevent destructive behavior, and safely confine her when you're busy. It is not a substitute for housebreaking, training, exercise, playtime or love. If Daisy spends most of her time in the crate, either your priorities are way off or you don't have the time or the desire for a puppy. Once your Dane is properly trained, the crate should become an open den that your dog uses when she's ready. Rarely should there be a need after puppyhood to confine her in the crate.

Housebreaking can be easy. Take Daisy to her designated toilet area after eating, drinking, napping and playing. She should also be taken out if she begins to sniff around like she might need to go. Take her out at least every two to three hours, even if she hasn't done any of the things that might signal a need. Walk her to the area, point to the ground and say "potty" or "hurry" or whatever command you wish to use, as long as the command is the same every time. At first she won't have the slightest idea what you expect, but give your command anyway. Stay with her until she does her business—do not remove her from the area until she's performed. When she starts to squat, calmly give

Your puppy's crate is a safe haven. Magic's Noel naps comfortably. Owned by Cathey Sohmer and bred by Linda Altomare, Magic Manor Danes, Hubbard, Ohio.

your command again. She will soon begin to associate the place, the command and the action. Then you've got a dog who knows where to go and what to do when she gets there. As soon as she performs, tell her "Oh good girl, potty, what a good girl!!!" Use an excited, happy voice and pop a little treat in her mouth at the same time.

All dogs prefer to be clean; they don't want to soil their living quarters. However, when you gotta go, you gotta go. By training her to go out to the potty area, you're allowing her to be clean, to learn self control and to please you.

If you catch Daisy making a mistake, make a loud "eck" noise and rush her to the potty area. Again, praise, praise, praise for performance. If you find an accident that has already happened, don't punish her. All you will gain is fear and confusion. Don't give any attention to the matter, either negative or positive. Remove her from the immediate vicinity, clean up the mess and use an odor eliminator. Watch her more closely to avoid future accidents. Never,

never hit her, and never rub her nose in her mess. She'll be scared and confused, and you may undo all the positive work you'd done before you lost your temper.

If you're very vigilant, Daisy should start to let you know when she needs out within several days. You'll have to learn her body language. Some dogs whine or bark, others stand quietly at the door or pace back and forth. Continue to accompany and praise her until there are no more accidents and you're sure she knows what to do. The whole process may take as little as a week, or as long as a couple of months.

If you're often not at home to let her out when necessary, install a doggy door in a damage-proof area such as the kitchen, and leave her there with her open crate when you're out. Some coaxing, a few treats and a lot of praise will have her using her own door in no time. The key to housebreaking is close supervision and lots of praise.

18

EXERCISE

Your Great Dane needs a specially planned exercise routine throughout his life. Most Danes are pretty calm and laid back indoors. If you have two dogs, they may get some of their exercise chasing each other around the backyard. Still, your Dane will need supervised walks and exercise every day once he's past his first year.

During Rover's first days with you, he'll get enough exercise running back and forth to the potty area and playing with the family. It's best not to venture out into the neighborhood until he's been checked by the vet and immunized. Don't hesitate to discuss his exercise needs with both your veterinarian and the breeder.

Once he's immunized and accustomed to a collar and leash, you can take short walks down the block once or twice a day. Intersperse the walks with short play and training sessions. Exercise can increase gradually as your Dane grows, but don't overdo. Forced exercise during growing periods could cause skeletal and joint problems. Many breeders advise that your puppy should be allowed to play and exercise only when he pleases. Limited exercise may be a factor in healthy bones and proper growth.

At around one year old, exercise can be gradually increased, providing your vet agrees that the increase is beneficial for your particular dog. By 18 months, your Dane should be developmentally mature enough for long walks, runs and lots of daily activity. Just remember, any changes

"Bumper," Can. Ch. Paquestone's V. Rolling Thunder CDX, TD, Can. CDX, TD, U-CD, ASCA-CD, WD, TDI has a unique method of exercising. Owned by Marta Brock, Olympia, Washington.

in his exercise routine should be approved by the vet.

Allow your puppy to play as he pleases. Disdain's A Dozer, owned by the author, enjoys his rope.

If you plan to compete in activities such as flyball, your dog must be conditioned gradually. Follow the guidelines for the activities in Section IV.

Once your Dane is fully grown—around two years old—his exercise should be increased for strengthening and protection of his cardiovascular system. Jogging beside a bike is an excellent choice (See Chapter 37), but have a complete physical exam done before beginning any endurance training. Your vet should rule out any skeletal or joint disorders as well as cardiac or circulatory problems.

Walhalla's Liebestraum CD, CGC takes his Min Pin friend, Ch. Siegreich's Danksgung V. J-T, CD, CGC, TDI out for a walk. Both dogs are owned by Chris and Henry Bredenkamp, Burleson, Texas.

Exercise can be fun as Disdain's A Dozer, Black Zeus of T's Mist and Michael McCracken can attest.

Again, your Dane must be conditioned slowly and gradually.

There are some basic exercise rules that should always be followed:

- Never exercise your Dane for one hour before and two hours after meals. You risk bloat, which can be deadly. (See Chapter 31)
- Avoid strenuous exercise on the weekends, with none during the week.
- Use proper caution in inclement weather. Be especially careful about summer exercise, which should be done in cooler early mornings and late evenings. Watch for signs of heat stress and fatigue.

Remember that daily walks and play sessions provide mental as well as physical stimulation. Slow down, relax and allow your Dane to enjoy his time with you and Mother Nature.

19

GROOMING

You should begin a grooming routine as soon as your Dane joins the family. Daily brushing will keep Daisy happier and healthier. She will look, feel and smell better, and be less likely to suffer from skin diseases and parasite infestations. The 10 to 15 minutes you spend brushing her will increase the bond between you, give you a chance to notice any lumps, bumps, cuts or bruises, and probably lower your blood pressure. That's right—interacting with your Dane is healthy for both of you!

The first few grooming sessions should be short and enjoyable. Let Daisy sniff the brush, then place her on a soft mat or towel, lying on her side. If she struggles, place your arm across her body and talk to her softly. Gently stroke her ears, encouraging her to lie still. Be very patient, and be sure to praise her as soon as she's still. Give little treats for good behavior. If she puts up a real struggle, tell her "No" in a firm, sharp voice. Again, praise and treat when she's still. Always make sure you have control before you begin to brush. If a struggle begins, regain control and start over. She'll soon realize that you're not going to hurt her, and that brushing feels good! She'll begin to look forward to her daily brushing sessions.

A natural bristle brush is fine for a Dane's short coat. You may want to try a curry comb made of pliable nubbed plastic for removing dead hair, or a hound glove, which is a mitt with a roughened palm surface, to remove dirt and massage the skin. Either will make her coat look clean and shiny.

Once a week, she will need a more complex grooming ritual, including ear and teeth cleaning and nail clipping. Again, use patience, firmness, praise and treats to get your puppy used to the routine. You should begin before she is 12 weeks old. During the week leading up to the first teeth cleaning, open her mouth several times a day and run your fingers gently over her teeth and gums for a few seconds. She should be comfortable with this handling before you begin to actually brush the teeth. As always, praise when she's quiet and accepting of the attention. Let her know she can look forward to a treat for being a good girl. When she's used to having her mouth handled, rub her teeth with a toothbrush designed for dogs or a piece of soft gauze bandage wrapped around your finger. Once she's comfortable with this, begin your weekly cleaning with dog toothpaste or a paste made from equal parts baking soda and salt with a little bit of water. You can continue to use gauze if it's easier than a brush. Use gentle, circular scrubbing strokes on all surfaces of the teeth, then rinse with water—a plant mister works great. Giving a few hard biscuits every day will make it easier to keep teeth clean.

Many Danes don't like to have their paws handled. Teach Daisy to accept this attention early in your relationship. Begin by holding and touching her paws several times a day. Gently touch the nails, inspect the pads, and separate the toes. Tell her what a wonderful girl she is; be patient and earn her trust. Then you can begin weekly nail clipping. You'll need a guillotine-type nail clipper designed for large dogs. The nails should be kept short so that the foot will remain compact and the toes will not splay. Longer nails reduce traction, cause an abnormal stance and gait, and can be painful. Clip only the white tip of the nail, avoiding the pink quick. Cutting into the quick causes pain and bleeding. If the nails are black, clip only a sliver at a time, beyond the curve of the nail. Keep styptic powder on hand for accidental bleeding. If you're unsure about nail clipping, ask your veterinarian to demonstrate.

Check the ears weekly for any signs of redness or discharge. A couple of drops of mineral oil will keep them clean.

If you notice reddened gums, ear discharge, a lump or swelling anywhere on the body, abraded footpads, or anything out of the ordinary, consult your veterinarian.

Many Great Dane breeders recommend only occasional bathing so as not to strip the coat of its natural oils. If necessary, bathing can begin at three to four months of age. You can have Daisy bathed at your vet's office or by a groomer, or pop her in the tub at home. Use a high quality shampoo recommended by your vet or breeder.

Assemble the shampoo, towels and other paraphernalia, and place a rubber mat in the tub to allow traction. Brush Daisy well, place cotton in her ears and a couple of drops of mineral oil in each eye, then place her in the tub, without water at first. Use lots of praise for cooperation, and a sharp "No" if she tries to get out. Wet her thoroughly with lukewarm water, about 93 degrees Fahrenheit. Apply shampoo, lather and rinse completely. A second application may be necessary if she is very dirty. Thorough rinsing is very important to prevent skin irritation. Towel dry well, and keep her in a warm, draft-free area until completely dry, making sure she does not become chilled.

A proper grooming routine will keep your Dane looking and feeling terrific, and you'll enjoy all the compliments you receive on your gorgeous companion!

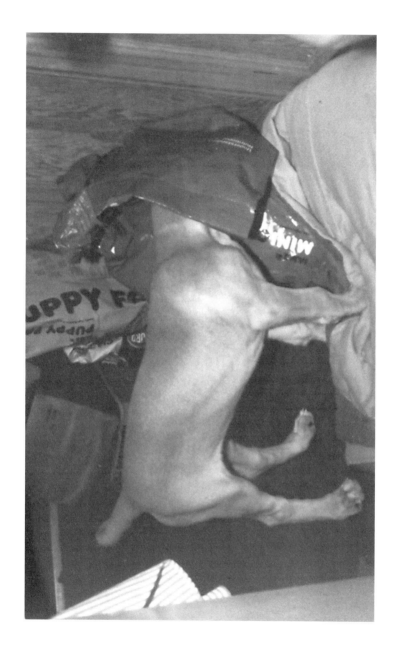

Brees' Pretty Miss Priscilla seems pretty happy with the food served at her house! "Cilla" is owned by Debbie Cole, Brees Danes, of Garland, Texas.

20

PROPER NUTRITION

Your Great Dane will eat a Great Deal! It is imperative that he be fed a balanced, nutritionally correct diet.

The breeder should have given you a small supply of food when you picked up Rover, along with information on feeding for the various stages of life. If you have done your homework and chosen a knowledgeable breeder, you may wish to stick with the diet she recommends.

Be very careful not to overfeed your pup. Many people mistakenly believe that by feeding more food to a puppy, he will mature into a larger dog. The adult size of your Dane is dependent primarily on genetics. Overfeeding Rover will put pressure and strain on developing bones and joints, often causing hip, elbow and shoulder problems.

Many breeders feel that too much protein may also cause developmental problems. Your breeder may advise you to feed your Dane an adult maintenance premium food, even as a puppy, to avoid the extra protein present in growth formulas. When choosing a food, look for a premium food with high digestibility. Most top breeders recommend foods with around 23% protein. You may also be advised to avoid foods with soy, beet pulp or ethoxyquin.

You will want to feed a dry premium food as the mainstay of Rover's diet. Picking a different brand of food each week, whether for convenience, price considerations or to prevent your Dane from becoming bored, is not advisable. You may wish to add small amounts of quality canned food or other meat, perhaps with a tablespoon or two of cool water to make a gravy, to enhance the flavor.

Changing your dog's basic diet could cause stomach upset or even bloat. (See Chapter 31). If you must change food brands, do so gradually. Mix the new food with the old in increasing proportion until the changeover is complete.

There are many nutritional supplements on the market. You may wish to discuss these with your breeder or

Ch. Von Shrado's I'm A Knock Out prefers name brand treats. "Fridge" lives with Jim and Sandy Hann, Von Shrado Danes, Pikeville, North Carolina.

veterinarian before giving them to Rover. Many Dane breeders suggest a vitamin C supplement, usually 500 mg/day for puppies and adolescents, and 1000 mg/day for adults. Some also add a little yogurt to their dogs' diets. This helps to encourage friendly bacteria which can improve digestion and vitality and may help with bloat.

From time to time, you may wish to offer treats to your Dane. Just remember that these should be kept to a minimum and should never be given as a substitute for time and affection. You may wish to consider uncooked knuckle or shank bones as "chew toys." They are reasonably priced, natural teeth-cleaners that will not splinter, and are sure to be a hit with your Dane.

As Rover grows, he will need raised food and water dishes. These should be about 19-20" off the floor when he is grown. Meals should be small and frequent. Small meals two to three times a day will help protect him from bloat. Never exercise your Dane or allow him to consume large amounts of water for at least an hour before or after meals. Feed at regular times when someone is home to observe him for an hour after eating. If you feed him right before you go to work and he bloats after eating, he may not live until you get home and get him to a veterinarian.

Dishes should have a permanent place, out of the way of loud noise and traffic. Make sure that fresh water is always available. Purified or filtered water is best. Consider adding a tablespoon of cider vinegar per bucket of drinking water. This may provide added protection against bloat.

Providing proper nutrition is one of the most important things you can do for your Great Dane.

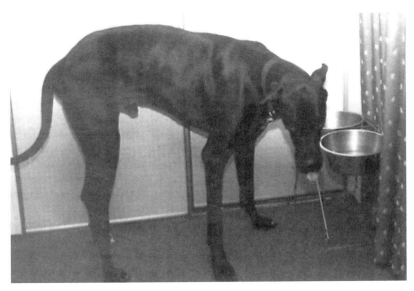

Consider raised food and water dishes.

MAKE YOUR OWN HEALTHY DOG TREATS

Begin with:

2 cups whole wheat flour
1 cup yellow cornmeal

Add any one or two of the following that may appeal to your Dane:

1/2 cup of brewers yeast
1/2 cup uncooked oatmeal
1/4 cup barley
1/4 cup shelled sunflower seeds
1/4 cup wheat germ

Choose a meat source:

3 beef or chicken bouillion cubes dissolved in 1 cup boiling water
1/2 lb. beef or chicken liver, pureed
1/2 cup beef or chicken stock
1/2 cup bacon drippings

Add one or two seasonings (wet seasonings may be better with beef or chicken liver, dry seasonings with other meat sources):

1 teaspoons garlic powder
1/2 teaspoon salt
1 egg
1/4 cup chopped parsley
2 tablespoons corn oil
1/4 cup lowfat milk
2 tablespoons parmesan cheese
2 tablespoons peanut butter (or use peanut butter in place of a meat source)

Finish with:

Added whole wheat flour or cool water to achieve desired "cookie dough" consistency.

Preheat oven to 350 degrees. Combine dry ingredients. Add wet ingredients and mix into a firm dough. Let sit for 15 minutes. Roll out on lightly floured surface to a 1/4 inch thickness. Cut into desired shape. If desired, cookies can be glazed with a mixture of one egg beaten with one tablespoon lowfat milk. Bake 25 to 30 minutes, or until golden brown and crunchy. Cool on wire rack. Store in airtight container.

Ch. Hope-N-Dagon's Flashy Hanna supervises all meal preparation. Owner Terry Beck, of Conroe, Texas, holds three-month-old Kasey Nichole Pace.

21

UNDERSTANDING YOUR DANE

Daisy will quickly become a member of the family, and you'll probably remark many times that she's "almost human." Indeed, you will have good reason to think so. She will quickly adapt to your sleeping times, activity periods, etc. You can look at her face and tell when she's happy or sad. She enjoys socializing, and seeks comfort and the "good life," just as you do. She shows joy, anger and jealousy. And, like you, she likes to know where she stands. She is happiest when she has a leader to admire and respect, or when she can be a leader herself.

Still, it's very important to realize that your Dane is a dog and that, despite the similarities, Daisy is very different from you. Your life with her will be much easier for both of you if you understand her dog nature.

In many ways, she is what man has made her. Her Dane ancestors were originally bred to battle boars, and to go to war; there is an element of aggression and dominance within her. She's big, strong and capable, and she knows it. But over the years, breeders worked to produce a "gentle giant" to be a companion to man. She wants to be close to you, and she will willingly subjugate herself—if you are deserving of her respect.

Despite the fact that her looks and temperament are mostly due to man's intervention, she retains many characteristics of her distant ancestor, the wolf. She is a predator, capable of tracking, hunting and killing her prey. The instinct to defend her territory is strong. She is a pack

Danes consider themselves a part of family life. CloudNine/FarHill Ca. Dreamn is a full-fledged family member at the home of Loleta and Doug Turner, CloudNine Danes, Eureka, California.

animal, needing a social heirarchy that lets her know who the pack leader is, and where she fits into the system. Because she considers the others in the household to be her pack, she will try very hard to communicate with you and to "play on your team." Understanding the various means of communication she uses will assist you in teaching her "pack rules" and helping her to be a productive family member.

She "talks" with her entire body. She'll tell you she wants to play with a bark or a play growl, perhaps running in circles or lowering her front legs and chest to the floor while sticking her rear end up in the air. She may show you her "play face," with her mouth relaxed and open, teeth exposed in a smile. If she's afraid, or simply submitting to your authority, she'll tuck her tail and try to appear small. If she's frightened enough to feel she must defend herself, she will probably growl or snarl along with laying back her ears and tucking her tail. She's telling you she will bite if you don't back off.

It is not true that a dog who is wagging her tail will not attack. If that wagging tail is being held upright, and is accompanied by growling, raised hackles, a wrinkled nose and bared teeth, you're in trouble. Hopefully, you will see only happy signals from your Dane, but it's best to recognize the not-so-happy ones as well.

Walhalla's Liebestraum CD, CGC enjoys a camping trip with Chris and Henry Bredenkamp, of Burleson, Texas.

A happy face is open, even silly looking. Worry can be seen in a wrinkled brow. If she wags her tail quickly and forcefully, she's being oh-so-friendly (but watch out for the tail!). A few slow wags when you speak to her says "I know you're here and I'm glad." A horizontal tail says everything's okay, but if it's tucked between her legs, she's unsure or afraid.

Daisy will seek the attention and approval of the person she considers pack leader. She needs you to feed and care for her, to play with her and teach her the rules. She does not like to be alone, and may be destructive if she's anxious or afraid. She may show her stress by chewing, barking, house soiling, or laying around looking bored. She needs to participate in family activities. Training and play will reduce both her stress and yours. Allow her to be useful, let her know how she fits into the family, motivate and reward her for proper behavior and she'll be a well-behaved, contented companion.

Your Great Dane should be a partner, separate and different, but deserving of your respect and understanding. If you work toward this goal, you will have a truly rewarding friendship with her that goes way beyond dog ownership.

A reward at the end of a training session. Zeus gently takes a tiny treat from Michael McCracken's mouth, while Dozer awaits his turn.

22

TRAINING YOUR DANE

You can have a wonderful bond with your Dane, or look back with regret at the day he came into your life. Much depends on the training you provide. Remember, Rover will only be as good as his training. Basic obedience is imperative. Both your safety and his may depend on it.

Training begins the day you bring him home. He will soak up knowledge like a sponge; there is no way to stop him from learning. It is, therefore, best to see that he gets a proper education, or he'll learn things you'd rather he didn't! It is very important that you train to the level of the dog. You can begin teaching a six week old pup his name, but don't expect him to obey difficult commands just yet.

The first important things for your puppy to learn are trust, housebreaking (See Chapter 17), socializing and his name. The first important thing for you to learn is that you never yell, hit, threaten, or otherwise abuse your Dane. Where there is pain and intimidation, there can be no learning—only fear. Your Dane cannot concentrate on learning if he is afraid of being hurt. As a kindergartener, if your teacher had told you "color the ball blue" and you colored it green, should she have yelled, hit you, and told you what a rotten kid you were? Would you have learned from the abuse? Yes—you would have learned that your teacher was out of control and to be afraid whenever she came near. Unfortunately, you still wouldn't know which color was blue. Likewise, if your dog scampers away when you say "sit," and you call him back and hit him, what will he learn? That you are out of control, undeserving of his respect, and that staying away from you is his best course of action. But, tell him "sit," show him how to sit, give him a treat when he sits, and tell him what a wonderful boy he is for sitting, and what will he learn? He'll learn that "sit" means to put his bottom on the floor, and he'll learn that obeying you is the smartest, safest, and most pleasant thing to do. Make training positive and you'll have a positive relationship with this big, sensitive guy for years to come.

The period between two and four months is extremely important. Begin dominance exercises so that your dog will accept you as pack leader. Again, dominance does not mean abuse. Dominance simply means that, just as with children, you are older and wiser and you make the rules. Frequently restrain your puppy for a few seconds at a time. Don't let go until he is still. Gently hold his muzzle closed for a second or two. Look into his face and hold the look until he averts his eyes. Remember, these are exercises for young puppies. If you have adopted a full grown Dane, best not to stare at him. If he should perceive this as a threat, you could be seriously injured. Use these exercises with your young puppy so that he will learn there is no threat and nothing to fear. Someday he may meet children at eye level—you want to be sure he doesn't think they are challenging him. Practice putting your hand in the food bowl while he is eating, perhaps adding food to the bowl a little at a time. Occasionally take a toy away, moving slowly and giving him every opportunity to submit gracefully to your authority.

If you already have a well-behaved adult dog in your home, she'll probably do some of your training for you. Adults will typically play with a puppy, and can be invaluable in teaching where to potty, when to bark, and when to back off and quit being a pest. It's best not to interfere if the adult growls at the pup or pins him to the floor. It is very rare for a grown dog to purposely injure a

CloudNine Echo V. Al Dawns Kahn learns to walk on a leash. Echo is owned by Loleta and Doug Turner, CloudNine Danes.

pup. She's simply teaching him the rules and exerting her higher authority.

From ten to sixteen weeks, you can begin leash training and start teaching the "sit" command. Training sessions should be short, about five minutes, and very upbeat. Don't allow your puppy to bite, jump on people, or do anything you will not allow when he's grown. Use treats and praise to teach him to come when you call, and to teach "watch me." Introduce him to car rides and to friendly people, but remember to keep him away from strange dogs until his immunizations are complete.

If puppy classes are available in your area, take advantage of the opportunity. Rover will be able to play and interact with other puppies, and be introduced to basic obedience commands at the same time. Choose a class based on treat and praise training, with no correction. You will learn a great deal about training methods while capitalizing on this important socialization period in your dog's life. If he is not exposed to other dogs and people during this time, he may grow up fearful, unfriendly, or even aggressive.

You may find puppy classes so helpful that you'll decide to continue formal training with your Dane. Group obedience classes teach Rover to pay attention in noisy, busy surroundings. Always observe a class before committing to a trainer. Make sure that none of the methods used make you uneasy, and that plenty of explanation and opportunity to practice is offered. You want a trainer who uses lots of praise, and hopefully has some experience with Danes. If you are unable to find a trainer, write to the National Association of Dog Obedience Instructors (NADOI). The address is listed in Appendix C. Some trainers specialize in comformation, tracking, or other canine pursuits. Once your Dane knows basic obedience commands, you can branch out into other types of training that will provide fun, exercise and social activity for both you and Rover (See Section IV). The more you train, the smarter your Dane will be, and the easier he will learn.

While training, remember these all-important reminders:

1. Socialize your Dane. Let him meet lots of dogs and people. Take him on car rides, walks in the park, visits to the homes of friends and relatives. Take along a few treats and try to make him comfortable in every new situation. Help him to relax and have fun, but insist on good behavior. You will raise a friendly, mannerly dog who will be welcome anywhere. Everyone will be saying, "I wish my dog would act like that!"

2. Use body language—yours and your dog's—to your advantage. Remember that Rover learns from nonverbal cues, such as your posture or tone of voice. Learning to use these assets can help you to communicate better. His body language can help you to read his intentions and avert bad behavior. If you notice he's about to jump on you, put him in a quick sit, then praise him. You needn't correct

him because he never had a chance to do anything wrong! If you're training your Dane and he cringes or cowers, you're being too tough—lighten up! But if he's slow to obey even though he knows the command well, stands tall with his tail up and a cocky, self-assured look on his face, you're being challenged. He's wondering if the boss is ripe for a takeover. Treat him firmly—NOT harshly—and insist he obey.

3. Training should be fun. Games like retrieving a ball, hide 'n seek, and the shell game (See Chapter 37) can all be used to teach obedience. The time you spend together will increase the bond between you, and Rover will not be bored and potentially destructive. Mixing training and fun makes for a more obedient—and happier—companion dog.

Nightwatch Fire N Ice V. Hogcreek CD learns to heel. This black male, owned by Susan and Herb Barney, Hogcreek Danes, has points toward his championship.

4. Reinforce good behavior. Make sure your timing is right, so that Rover understands just what you're so pleased about. A treat, a walk, a toy, a hug—if given at the right time, these things will convince your dog that pleasing you is to his advantage. If he whines and you give him a biscuit to shut him up, what's he going to do the next time he'd like a biscuit? You got it—he's going to whine some more! That's called the dog training the person! But if you insist he "Hush! Sit!," then give a biscuit, he will learn that, in order to get what he wants, he must first do what you want. The behavior you reward is the behavior you encourage.

5. Motivate your dog. He wants to please you, and he'll want to even more if he associates you with praise, treats, fun and love. Encourage and reward good behavior even when you're not in a "training session." Puppies who receive a lot of stimulation are more receptive to learning later on. He will consistently obey you if you make sure he understands the lesson and make it fun. His confidence blossoms with your approval.

6. No, he's not stupid and, yes, he can hear! Let's say you've been working in the backyard for days, practicing the "sit" and "down." Rover responds reliably on command. So you go next door to show off, bragging about how quickly he has learned. You say "sit" and he continues to stand and look around. "Rover, sit." No response. "Did you hear me, Rover? I said sit down, right now!" Still nothing. What went wrong here? Is he deaf or just stupid? Neither one. He's confused. After working for days, he learned to sit and down on command. And he associated those commands with something the two of you do alone in the backyard every day. Why does he do it? To please you, and

to get a treat, a game or a hug. How do these commands fit into his life? He doesn't have the slightest idea—yet. He only knows that he's in a strange place with people standing over him, and he's not at all sure what to do. Put yourself in his place. You may sing Tina Turner songs to your bathroom mirror, but could you prance up on stage in front of an audience without fear? When your puppy looked to you for guidance, you made it worse. Instead of enforcing the "sit" command, you began to get irritated and embarrassed, maybe even yelled a little, and started adding words that he didn't understand. You even said "sit down." Which do you want—sit or down? Rover's not the one who's not learning his lessons here! Use one command to mean one thing—religiously. If today, "down" means "lie down," tomorrow "down" can't be used to mean "get down off the couch." To remove him from the furniture, teach "off." And

"Sit!" Diamond's Leather and Lace CGC (in the center) learns to sit at an obedience class. He is owned by Jill Zondervan and Shelley Hayse, of San Jose, California.

don't confuse the issue with a lot of "did you hear me" and "do what I tell you." Use proper commands in a firm, clear voice. Give a command once, then enforce it if he doesn't obey. Remember that his hearing is about 16 times more acute than yours, so there's no need to be loud or to keep saying things over and over. You can be sure he heard you, but are you sure he understood you? Show him what to do; enforce the command. Remember that it is easier to show him what to do than to show him what not to do.

7. You must be consistent. Things that are not allowed are not allowed—period. This should include growling at you, resisting your handling, snapping and any other attempt at dominating you. It may also include sleeping on your bed and trying to catch the cat's tail. Once you decide what's not okay, let your dog know to cease and desist immediately each and every time he does it. When he jumps on the couch—"No! Off!" Use a firm voice as you remove him from the couch. Then use a positive voice to say "Good boy! Off!" If you use the same rules and commands consistently, you will earn your Dane's respect. Remember that, in his world, every pack has a leader. Consistency is the key to making sure you are the leader of this pack.

8. Be a good role model. Teach Rover how to respond to stressful situations by demonstrating the right response. If he is frightened the first time he visits the vet, behave in a positive, upbeat manner and he will learn to do the same. If there is fear in your voice as you talk with the vet, or if you tell the pup "Oh, poor baby, it's okay" when he gets a shot, he'll get the idea that there's plenty to be upset about. Act happy, not nervous. He will take his cue

from you. If you must leave him at home alone, treat it as a normal course of events. Don't tell him "It's okay, I'll be back; I'm not going to leave you!" What you will provide is fear, not reassurance. When you come home, it's great to greet each other in a loving, friendly manner, but don't overdo the sentiment. You don't want him to be nervous or anxious every time you go out or come in. What do you say to other family members when you return home? Probably "Hi, I'm home!" Maybe they even get a quick kiss, but you don't run to them saying "It's okay now! I came home to you. See, I told you I wouldn't leave you! Don't worry!" They would think something was definitely wrong if you went overboard trying to convince them that everything was okay. So will your dog. Whenever Rover is unsure, behave the way you want him to behave.

9. Think like a dog. He's a very intelligent animal, but he's not human. Behaviors handed down to him by his wolf ancestors, such as chasing prey, are not appropriate in his life with you. You must teach him that modifying his behavior is to his advantage. Use his natural needs for food, leadership and companionship as training advantages.

10. Training is forever. You can teach Rover to sit, but if you don't use the command for six months, he's going to forget. Commands should be used, not just for training sessions, but in your everyday life. Give him a chew toy and tell him "down/stay" when you want to watch a TV program. Tell him "sit/stay" when the doorbell rings. Have him "heel" when you cross a busy street. Not only will your Dane be a joy to live with, he will feel secure and happy.

"Down, Stay!" CloudNine/FarHill Ca. Dreamn demonstrates these commands. Owned by Loleta and Doug Turner, CloudNine Danes, Eureka, California.

The same basic rules apply if you have adopted an older dog. But keep in mind that there are probably a lot of things about your dog and his upbringing that you do not know, especially if he is a rescue dog. Before you begin formal training, give him a chance to know and trust you. Let him get used to your daily routine. Let him know that you are the source of his food. Play gently with him; take him for long walks and car rides and talk, talk, talk to him. Touch him gently but firmly, and let him know you will not hurt or punish him. Be consistent about the rules, and patiently teach him what you expect. Start positive training sessions when you feel the dog has begun to bond with you. Always reward for good behavior, and use lots of praise, patience and persistence. If you are ever afraid or insecure about training your adult Dane, consult a professional trainer immediately.

Whether you are training a puppy or an adult, there are some very important commands that every dog should learn.

1. "Watch me." With Rover sitting in front of you, place a treat in front of his nose so that he can smell it. Move the treat to your face, saying "watch me." When he looks at you, say "good boy" and give the treat immediately. Practice each day until he automatically looks at you on command. "Watch me" is invaluable for getting your dog's attention.

2. From "watch me," it's easy to proceed to leash walking. First fasten the leash to Rover's buckle collar and let him drag it around the house—with your supervision, of course. When he's comfortable with the leash, use treats to teach him to follow you. Tell him "watch me" and reward for performance. Then, holding the leash loosely, maintain eye contact and back away to the end of the leash. If he follows you, give him a treat. Soon he will be following you each time you back away. Begin to back up further, encouraging him gently to move with the leash and rewarding when he does. As soon as he's reliably following the leash, back away, then turn and walk forward with the pup by your left side. Maintain eye contact, say "watch me, heel" and treat for proper performance. You'll be teaching "heel" in greater detail later on.

3. "Sit." With Rover on leash, hold a treat closed up in your hand where he cannot see it. Hold your hand in front of his nose, then move it up and back, going over his head toward his rear at an angle. Use the "sit" command, keeping the leash snug so that he cannot back up. When he can't raise his head any further while standing up, he will likely sit so that he can keep the hand in sight. As soon as he sits, say "good boy, sit" and give the treat.

4. "Okay" is really a release word rather than a command. It means we're finished with what we were doing. Whenever you give a command, you'll want Rover to know when you no longer expect him to sit, stay or whatever. An upbeat "okay" will release him from the command.

5. "Come" should mean "come here for good things" like praise, treats, hugs, etc. Never call your dog for correction or punishment—never, no matter what! To teach, choose a time when Rover is a little tired and doesn't need to go to the bathroom. Put him on a long lead and let him wander around. Once something has captured his attention, say "Rover, come" and give a little tug on the lead. Encourage him at first with hand clapping, stooping down to his level. Reel him in with the leash if necessary. When he gets to you, meet him with open arms and a treat. He must obey the "come" command every time, for his own safety. If he should get away from you, and doesn't respond to the "come" command, resist the urge to chase him. He will think it's a game and run all the more. He will also learn that he can run faster than you! Best to keep that piece of information to yourself! Call his name excitedly and tell him "watch me." Once you have his attention, back away from him, calling his name and making it a game for him to chase you. You'll get him back much quicker this way. To make it even easier to teach "come," shake a box of dog treats as you give the command. He'll learn very quickly that "come" means "cookie."

6. Before you teach the "heel" command, keep in mind that it's not always necessary to walk in a perfect heel formation. Relaxed walks should be just that— relaxed. Take time to smell the roses—or the fire

hydrants. Remember that your Great Dane is not a robot. However, heeling is used to get you safely through crowded streets, and will keep Rover focused on you whenever necessary. You'll also avoid being pulled down the street—and this big guy can certainly pull—whenever he spots a perky Poodle or a sassy Samoyed. You want him to walk happily by your left side, not forging ahead or lagging behind, keeping up with you on a loose lead. Hold the leash with your right hand, which should be resting against your midsection. The leash should hang loosely between the two of you. Use your left hand only when necessary to make corrections. With Rover in a "sit" by your left side, give the "heel" command and step off with your left foot. As you go along, remind him to "watch me" and praise him when he's walking by your side. If he's not paying attention, quickly pop the leash in a slightly downward motion and change direction. Then praise him for catching up to you! He will soon learn that if he doesn't watch you closely, you may take off in any direction! If he lunges ahead, quickly turn in the opposite direction and keep walking, encouraging him to return to his proper "heel" position. Work on keeping his interest. Once he's used to the idea, use plenty of square right and left turns. Correct with a leash pop if necessary, but never correct if Rover's paying attention and staying where he's supposed to be. When turning left, you will be stepping right in front of him and may even bump him. He will learn quickly that he gets run into if he's even slightly too far ahead. Never deliberately step on your Dane, but don't walk around him either. Just bump into him if necessary, being careful not to fall over him and injure either of you, and continue to walk. It's his job to pay attention and turn when you turn. Make it interesting and fun—talk to him,

Big D's Blue Ox Babe CDX and nine-year-old Stephanie Scott are part of the 4-H Top Dog Drill Team. Owned by Susan and Herb Barney, Hogcreek Danes, Pearland, Texas.

praise him a lot, and make sure he pays attention. Speed up or slow down, correcting only if he fails to match your stride. Make it a game and praise him for every correct response! If he lags behind, simply speed up. A correction here could cause him to lag even more. Give him praise as you speed up and praise him even more when he catches up to you. When you stop, such as at a curb, have him sit. When you step off, give the "heel" command.

7. It may take a lot of work to teach your Dane to "Stand." When he is sitting, place a treat in front of his nose, then move your hand forward. Give the command when he stands to let his nose follow the treat. Take up the slack in the leash to stop him in the stand, giving him treats, praise and petting. Talk to him warmly and use your hands to keep him steady.

8. To teach your dog to lie quietly, use the "down" command. Hold a treat in front of his nose, give the command and move your hand in a downward motion to the floor. As his nose follows the treat, move it forward so that he must lie down to follow the treat. If he attempts to keep his belly off the floor, place your left hand on his back to encourage him to "down" completely. As soon as he is down, reward and praise his efforts.

9. You will want to use the "stay" command in conjunction with "sit," "stand" and "down." "Stay" simply means "don't move from that position until I tell you it's okay." Place Rover in the position you want him to hold, give the command, step in front of him and face him. Stand quietly for about five seconds. If he moves, tell him "no" and place him back in position. Again give the command and step away. Give him a treat and praise for holding the position for a few seconds. This command takes time to learn. Use short, upbeat sessions and keep your attitude positive. Only after he obeys consistently should you increase the amount of time he is to stay or the distance you move away from him. Eventually, you want to be able to tell your dog to stay, walk away, and have him hold the position until you return. If your dog must stay for more than a couple of minutes, use "stay" in conjunction with "down" for his comfort. Remember, "stay" cannot be used as a substitute for play, exercise and affection. You should not expect your Dane to remain in a set position for long periods.

10. "Off." When your 25 pound puppy jumps on you, you are likely to laugh and pet him, pleased that he is seeking your attention. When your 150 pound

dog jumps on you, knocking you to the ground, you won't be quite so pleased. You prevent the latter by not allowing the former. If your Dane is a jumper, keep him on leash during times you expect him to jump, such as when the kids come home from school. Hold the leash up close to his collar, but keep it loose. When he goes to jump, calmly give the "off" command, snapping to the side and down on the leash. The correction should put him slightly off balance, causing him to put his feet back on the floor. As soon as he drops to the floor, praise him, but not in an excited voice that might convince him to jump again. Then give another command, such as "sit," followed by the praise and attention he was looking for in the first place. If he jumps on you when he's not on a leash, cross your arms over your chest and look away, ignoring him completely. This will confuse him and he'll probably drop back to the floor and look at you. When he does, praise him and put him in a "sit," then give him the attention he is after.

11. "Drop it." Your Dane may pick up all kinds of things that you'd rather he didn't, from a soiled diaper, dropped in a parking lot, to a dead rat to broken glass. Once he's got it, it's too late to tell him to "leave it," so he must also understand "drop it." With Rover on a leash, give him a large-sized toy. As you hand it to him, say "Rover, take it" and praise him for holding it. Then lean forward a little bit, make eye contact and tell him "drop it." (Note: Do not make eye contact with an adult dog that you do not know well or feel totally confident with. It may be perceived as a threat and could precipitate an attack.) Hold an end of the toy, without pulling, and snap the leash downward. Use a quick snap and release. You may have to snap more than once to get him to open his mouth. As

soon as he relaxes pressure on the toy, move it out of sight and tell him what a wonderful boy he is! Repeat the exercise frequently, praising him profusely when he begins to loosen his grip. When he willingly drops the toy every time, begin to use the command with other things he likes, slowly working your way up to great, wonderful things like tennis balls and hot dogs. Be generous with your praise, or he'll definitely choose the hot dog! If your Dane ever appears to be even considering aggression, stop and consult a professional trainer immediately.

12. The "leave it" command means "back off and leave it alone immediately." This is the best way to keep him from picking up that dead rat in the first place. It can also keep him from chasing kids on bikes or the neighbor's cat. To teach "leave it," put Rover

"Was that good?" Nightwatch Fire N Ice V. Hogcreek asks Susan Barney.

on a leash and have treats at hand. Toss a treat several feet away, saying "Rover, leave it." If he lunges for the treat, snap the leash sideways and release. The second he stops moving toward the treat, tell him what a good dog he is and give him a treat from your hand. Retrieve the first one and try again. You can also teach him "okay, take it" and let him go after the tossed treat if you choose. Work up slowly to more prized treats, placing them closer and closer. Cut back on treats gradually, taking him on walks and telling him "leave it" when he starts to pick up used chewing gum or a discarded fast food bag. Always—ALWAYS give him lots of praise for obedience.

Not only are these basic commands necessary for the safety and comfort of you and your dog, they are the foundation upon which future learning is built. They will also help you with many of the special problems Dane owners encounter. A Dane trained to "heel" won't be pulling you into traffic or causing you to fall. Teach him "off" and he won't be one of the many Danes that hurt and frighten people by jumping on them forcefully. If he knows how to "stand" or "sit," he won't be leaning against you and pushing you over, something many Danes have been known to do.

Using fun, praise and treats as motivators, you can go on to teach Rover many things. It may be "bait and stack" for conformation (see Chapter 33) or "front and finish" for obedience competition (see Chapter 35). You can teach him to relay race, pick up his toys and play hide 'n seek (see Chapter 37). The more you teach him, the more you increase the bond between you, and the more you will bring out his most positive traits—and yours.

23

PROBLEM SOLVING

If you've consistently followed the training advice in Chapter 22, you shouldn't have many behavior problems with your Great Dane. There are, however, a few things you should know about the typical Dane.

She's a leaner. When you stand next to her, she's likely to lean against you and let you support her weight. If you are strong enough to hold her up and you don't mind, fine. But if anyone else is expected to walk or care for her, it's best not to let her leaning become a habit. Once a habit is developed, a Dane doesn't let go of it easily. Take a side step, give the "stand" command, and praise her for standing on her own. No matter what you are teaching, the same training principles apply.

The first time she backs up and sits on the couch—looking decidedly human—you will no doubt be amused. If you don't object to her being on the furniture, wonderful, but remember—there's no difference in jumping on the couch and stretching out or backing up to sit demurely—she's still on the furniture! Also keep in mind that backing up to sit on the couch leads to backing up to sit in your lap! Many Dane owners love it, but if you don't, enforce the rules. Tell her "off" followed by another command such as "sit." Reward and praise her for being where she's supposed to be.

If your Dane is somewhat dominant, you may find her bumping into you when you try to walk. She may be

Many Danes tend to be leaners, as Nightwatch Fire N Ice V. Hogcreek demonstrates. This pointed dog is owned by Susan and Herb Barney, Hogcreek Danes, Pearland, Texas.

trying to get your attention, to move you in a different direction or simply to push you around a little. She probably bumps in a friendly, even affectionate manner, but if you let her move you from your intended course or make you walk around her, you're teaching her that she's in charge. Your Dane should always be treated with the utmost love and respect, but should never be allowed to be a bully— not even a friendly one! She can't push you around if she's in a "down/stay," so use your commands and remember to praise, praise, praise for good behavior.

Danes are notorious for jumping on people and for pulling you down the street when you try to walk them on a leash. Be on the lookout for these tendencies and use the training advice given for these problems in Chapter 22.

The Great Dane has a wonderful tendency to protect her family, but over-protectiveness can be scary and dangerous. Lots of early socialization is the best preventive measure. If she is still over-protective, seek professional help to assist you in teaching her proper role in the family. If you encourage dominance and over-protectiveness in your puppy, you may end up with a very large dog that you are unable to control.

You may face other "doggie" problems with your Dane. Chewing is expected in teething puppies of any breed, but a Dane pup left unsupervised can unstuff your entire couch! Utilize the crate as described in Chapter 17, and make sure she has plenty of toys to chew. Keep in mind that incessant barking, digging, chewing, etc. are often signs of stress, loneliness and boredom. To alleviate the problem, you must alleviate the underlying cause. Inclusion in family activities is likely to chase away the blues and the bad behavior.

You may still run into an occasional behavior problem, but most can be prevented, and almost all solved. Keep in mind that dogs learn at different rates, just as people do. Some catch on quickly, but forget easily; others learn at a slower pace, but may have better retention. You may be lucky enough to have a Dane who soaks up knowledge at an amazing rate and has a memory like an elephant! Regardless of which category your particular Dane fits into, stick with it! Don't despair if it seems that Rover and training are like oil and water. One day, in the not-too-distant future, you'll watch a neighbor being hauled down the street by his very large dog, trying to hold onto both his dog and his dignity. You'll snicker and say to yourself,

"I'd never let MY dog behave like that!" and you'll suddenly realize that good ol' Rover really did learn to behave somewhere along the way. You may not even realize when it happened, but happen it did! You'll say to a family member, "Remember when we thought he'd never even learn to sit?" Perhaps you'll even have a chat with your neighbor about consistency, motivation and praise. "Hang in there," you'll advise, "It works every time!"

Jumping can be a problem with Danes. Henry Bredenkamp, though, loves the hugs he gets from Siegreich's Amstel V. Nahallac CDX, CGC, Siegreich Danes, Burleson, Texas.

24

YOUR DANE AS A FAMILY MEMBER
AND GOOD NEIGHBOR

Virtually all Great Danes live with one or more adults who have primary responsibility for the care and control of the dog. Many Danes also live with other dogs, cats and children. Most have close neighbors that could be frightened or disturbed by bad behavior. It is up to you to see that the others in your dog's life both give and receive proper respect.

The typical Dane is a great companion for older children, but may be too large and clumsy for infants and toddlers. He has a natural protective instinct and a tolerant nature. He's big and not as easily injured as a small dog might be. Still, to live with children, he must be very well trained. You must stress that the dog is to be gentle with the children at all times, and vice versa!

Children must be taught that Rover is a loving friend and playmate, but not a horse to be ridden or a stuffed toy to be mauled. Your Dane has a right to love and respect. You can and should expect him to be gentle and tolerant with your children; you cannot expect him to tolerate being teased, hit or in any way mistreated. To allow your child to abuse the dog is to risk serious injury to the dog. To believe that your Dane—or any dog—will not eventually retaliate against the abuser is to risk serious injury, even death, to the child.

The adults in the home must be the responsible parties—period. Even an older child cannot be solely

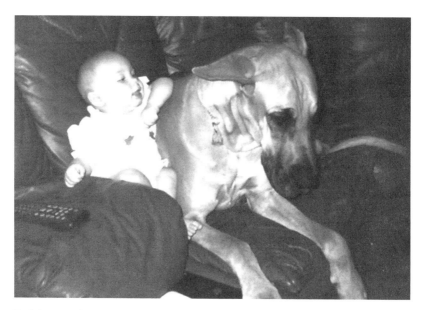

Babies and dogs should be carefully supervised, but Danes are usually tolerant. Ch. Hope-N-Dagon's Flashy Hanna is devoted to 10-month-old Kasey Nichole Pace.

responsible for the care and training of a dog—particularly a giant dog. A 12-year old walking a Dane alone could be beset by situations in which he or she would be unable to control the typically well-behaved Dane. Should Rover feel the need to protect himself or the child from a perceived aggressor, serious injury or death—to your child or dog, or perhaps to someone else's child or dog —could be the result.

Remember that children learn best by watching you. If you are patient and gentle with your Dane, your children are likely to follow your example. Include the kids and the dog in activities with you; praise both for good behavior and cooperation. Help them to love and to trust each other. Always keep in mind that your Dane is likely to protect your children—supervise any young visitors they may have at all times! Rover could misunderstand another child's intentions, or decide to interfere in an innocent tussle over a toy. If your child's friends are unreliable or unknown to your Dane, or if you have any reason to believe that Rover could be unreliable with other children, don't take any chances! Separate the dog to a place where the kids cannot go!

Having more than one dog in the family can be wonderful if you are patient and prepared. They can provide company and exercise for each other when you are otherwise occupied. You must let each dog know that you are the pack leader. Make sure that the first dog gets extra love and attention, and knows that she is not being displaced in your affections. Allow her to show the newcomer the ropes, but not to intimidate. Only interfere if you must, and then by redirecting their activity if possible. If it appears that an altercation is eminent, involve both dogs quickly in a training session. Make sure each has his own dishes, bed and toys. They will probably trade and share later on, but let them decide when the time is right. Make sure each has an opportunity to spend time away

Most Danes get along well with cats. Future Ch. Maitau's Who's The Boss snuggles with Cajun the kitty. Boss, owned by Patricia Ciampa and Helen Cross, Maitau Danes, is four months old here.

143

from the other, and that each receives individual attention.

Be very cautious about bringing in an adult dog with a resident adult, especially if they are the same sex. This is an introduction best done by a very experienced dog person! Opposite sex dogs are more likely to be agreeable, and it's best if the new dog is a youngster. Make sure all adults are spayed and neutered. While many Danes live well with much smaller dogs—even Chihuahuas—giants tend to live best with other very large dogs.

Most Danes live well with cats. Make sure that your puppy knows early that chasing the cat is strictly off limits! If you have an older cat, much of the success of the relationship will depend on the cat. Some will never accept a dog. In this instance, you can only supervise closely, make sure they have their own space to retreat from each other, and keep them separated when you're not around. Again, the dog is never to chase the cat, and the cat's nails should be kept trimmed short for the safety of the dog. If you are adopting an adult Dane, proceed with extreme caution until you know how he feels about cats! If he's never been exposed to cats, he may consider them prey! Introducing a kitten to a household with a Dane in residence is usually pretty easy. Danes accept most babies well, be they canine, feline or human. Just make sure the kitten is not accidentally injured by those big paws! A kitten and a Dane pup growing up together will probably become the best of friends. Always make sure that each has his own space and possessions, and receives individual attention.

If there are other pets in your household—rabbits, hamsters, gerbils, mice, ferrets, snakes, turtles, birds, etc.—make sure that they are secure and protected from your Dane or any other dog.

Since your Dane is an indoor dog, he shouldn't be much of a bother to the neighbors. Still, there are reasonable guidelines to be followed. Never let your Great Dane run loose. When you go for a walk, never let him use the neighbor's yard as a toilet area. If he potties in a public

Well-behaved Danes are welcomed in the community. Marta Brock's Rolling Thunder Danes and her Samoyed are always welcome.

area, clean it up! You should also clean up any messes in your own yard frequently to prevent insects and odor. Realize that your neighbors don't want the odor of dog droppings wafting on to their property, nor do they wish to listen to your dog bark all night. If you respect their rights to cleanliness, quiet and privacy, they will most likely respect your right to keep a companion Dane—or two or three!

Keep your dog's shots and license up to date, train him to be obedient and keep him under control—your neighbors will think he's a great addition to the community!

Generations of wonderful companions. Ch. Maitau's Topper Junior (3 yrs.), Ch. Maitau's Top Billing (4 1/2 yrs.), Maitau's Village Gossip (7 yrs.), Ch. Maitau's Tattletale (10 yrs.) and Ch. Maitau's Conversation Piece (12 yrs.). All are owned by Helen Cross and Patricia Ciampa.

25

THE AGING DANE

There is a wonderful Swiss expression that is used to describe the Bernese Mountain Dog, but is equally applicable to the Great Dane. "Three years a young dog, three years a good dog, and three years an old dog. All else is a gift from God." It is unfortunate but true that, by the age of six, your wonderful companion Dane—who was a puppy just yesterday—is going gray around the muzzle and showing definite signs of aging. Our Danes don't typically have the longevity that many breeds enjoy. While enthusiasts find this the saddest part of Dane ownership, we are in agreement that we'd rather share nine quality years with a Dane than twenty with another breed.

In preparation for your Dane's geriatric years, you should increase his preventive health care around his fifth birthday. Veterinary checkups should be scheduled every six months instead of the previous once a year. Proper nutrition becomes even more important. Providing your Dane with healthy nutrients and antioxidants may even add years to his life.

While your Dane is still relatively young and healthy, you can ask your vet to establish baseline blood and urine levels to serve as a comparison later on. You will then want to be on the lookout for changes in your dog. Work closely with your vet to determine which changes are warning signs of illness, and which are simply part of the natural aging process. You should observe his eating and drinking habits, note any changes in urine output or bowel

Good care and grooming become even more important for older Danes. Brett's Instanz V. Siegreich CDX, TDI shows gray on her muzzle and most of her hair. She is owned by the Bredenkamps.

movements, and monitor his attitude and stamina level.

Serious problems such as cancer, heart disease, and kidney or liver trouble are more likely to crop up in a geriatric dog. Watch for problems such as weight loss, poor appetite, increased thirst and urination, digestive problems, tiredness, lameness, coughing and shortness of breath. Check frequently for lumps, sores, discharge from any body orifice, odor from ears or mouth, and parasites. Early diagnosis and treatment of health problems can make all the difference in both quality and quantity of life.

Little things that have always been important become absolutely necessary. Your Dane should be groomed on a regular basis, and his teeth kept clean and free of tartar. Vaccinations should be given religiously to help protect the immune system.

As your Dane ages, his need for both care and understanding may increase. He will need as little stress as possible in his life. He will depend more and more on his comfortable daily routine. You should certainly continue the activities that he enjoys, but walks in the park may need to be taken with more leisure as he gets older. Always keep the concept of "quality" uppermost in your mind. Your oldster will enjoy catching his squeaky toy as you toss it across the living room in the same way he enjoyed chasing it across the yard when he was younger. His abilities may diminish, but his love for both you and that favorite squeaky toy is stronger than ever.

Rover may become less alert as time goes by, and may even experience problems with his vision or hearing. You may not even notice until he no longer comes when you call, or trips over a new piece of furniture. Try to be alert for these changes. He may need to urinate more frequently. Some older dogs just can't "hold it" as long as they could in their prime. Don't get mad at the occasional break in housetraining, and never fail to give him fresh water. Just

The muzzle of Dagmar's Martina is beginning to gray. She is owned by Penny and Rick Garcia.

make sure the problem is truly "old age" and not diabetes or another treatable medical malady. Some dogs become more grouchy and irascible with time, and don't appreciate loud parties, bouncy visitors or anything unusual. Once your Dane is truly old, you'll want to refrain from adding a new puppy to the house, or boarding an aging Rover while you visit Europe for a month.

Though Danes seldom live long enough to reach true senility, your dog may still need extra reassuring touches and pats. He may be slightly disoriented if he wakes suddenly during the night. Consider providing soft light or allowing him to sleep in your bedroom at night. He should be given a soft bed in a warm, quiet, draft-free indoor spot on the ground floor. Keep in mind that arthritis may slow him down a lot, but that much can be done to treat the discomfort and to retard the progress of the disease.

If your Dane becomes ill, discuss your options carefully with your veterinarian before deciding to hospitalize him. Some things can only be done in a hospital setting, but others can be dealt with at home where your dog feels the safest and most loved. If your Dane faces constant pain that can't be alleviated, or a debilitating illness that is certain to claim his life in the end, you may be confronted with the question of whether or not to end his suffering. The decision to euthanize your much-loved companion is a horrible one to have to make but, again, the watchword is "quality." You know Rover so well, and only you can decide if the last kind and loving thing you can, and should, do for him is to let him go.

Regardless of how the end comes, the loss of your Dane will be a tremendous one. When you lose a loved one, the grief is intense and can be devastating, whether that loved one is a person or a dog. There are many good books to help you work through your feelings of depression, anger, and sadness. It may help to talk to someone, either a professional or just another "dog person" who understands how you feel.

You'll never be able to replace your old friend, but a new Dane may help to fill the empty places in your day and your heart. Only you will know when, and if, the time is right to add a new pet to your life. In the meantime, hold close the love you shared with Rover. You may want to write down all the cute things he did, or gather up all your photos and make a special album in tribute to him. Remember that others in your family, both people and pets, will be missing Rover also. Try to help them through this difficult time, and allow them to help you as well. Hang on to the knowledge that grief fades with time, but the happy memories you shared will live forever in your heart. In spite of all the hurt, you were so lucky to have had this wonderful friend in your life. Dog lovers will tell you that Rover waits for you "just over the rainbow bridge." After all, heaven just wouldn't be heaven without our best friends.

SECTION III

THE HEALTH OF YOUR DANE

That first visit to the veterinarian is vitally important. This is adorable Magic's Stairway to Heaven, owned by Tom and Kathy Hinson and bred by Linda and Mike Altomare, Magic Manor Danes, Hubbard, Ohio.

26

THE FIRST VISIT TO THE VETERINARIAN

If you followed advice on choosing a good breeder, you probably have a health guarantee on your pup, with 72 hours or so after purchase in which to take Daisy for her first vet visit.

Although this first visit won't take more than an hour or two, it is very important in many ways. You want to determine first of all that your pup has no detectable genetic problems at this stage of her life that would necessitate returning her to the breeder. You want to know that there are no serious pest or parasite infestations, skin problems, infections or nutritional deficiencies. Once she receives a reasonably clean bill of health, you want to begin her all-important vaccination program. Furthermore, you want to forge a positive working relationship with the veterinarian and staff for both you and your dog.

Understand that the veterinarian cannot promise that Daisy will never suffer a serious illness or genetic disease. The onset of many such problems are later in life, with no indications at an early age. However, the doctor can check for evident congenital defects of the heart, eyes, bone structure, etc. He will look for ear mites, intestinal worms, fleas and ticks. If you have noticed any potential problems, such as a runny nose, eye discharge, persistent scratching, head shaking or diarrhea, be sure to let the doctor know.

The vet will begin a series of vaccinations to protect Daisy from a number of illnesses. Make sure you receive a schedule for follow-up exams and further inoculations. Ask your vet when your Dane will be protected enough to participate in puppy classes or otherwise meet the public, and at what age heartworm preventive should be started.

If your pup's ears are cropped, have the vet make sure they are healing properly. If you are planning to crop, discuss your intentions (See Chapter 10).

Discuss also your Dane's exercise and nutritional needs. Tell the doctor what advice the breeder gave you for feeding and exercise. Be sure to let him know if the breeder suggested any vitamin or nutritional supplements.

Don't be afraid to ask questions. The more you and the veterinarian talk and share information, the more Daisy will benefit. It often helps to make a list of any questions or concerns before you visit the vet, so that nothing is forgotten. There are many important things that you need to know that the doctor can demonstrate for you—giving pills, taking a temperature, and nail clipping, for instance. Make sure that you know how to reach your veterinarian or emergency clinic after hours.

You can expect the vet to be friendly with Daisy, but probably not to coo over how sweet, pretty, smart and wonderful she is. Better that the doctor take an interest in how healthy she is. The veterinarian is a health professional, and will treat your dog in much the same professional manner as your doctor treats you. Remember also that Daisy will respect firm, friendly, matter-of-factness much more than baby talk and kisses.

Keep in mind that your puppy's attitude toward vet visits will likely reflect yours. She's probably not going to be afraid or worried if she's pretty sure you're relaxed and comfortable. Act the way you want her to act. Take along a few treats, encourage her to relax, and make vet visits an adventure! Not everything that happens at the clinic will be fun, but it needn't be frightening. After all, this place and these people are going to be an important part of your life with your Dane.

27

BASIC VETERINARY CARE

Health maintenance and preventive care are among the most important things you do for your dog. While many of his basic health needs will be met in the home (see Chapter 28), regular examinations by a good veterinarian are imperative.

Religiously follow your vet's schedule for inoculations and checkups. It costs much less to prevent problems than it does to cure them. Rover should have up-to-date vaccinations against canine distemper, parvovirus, hepatitis, leptospirosis and rabies. Discuss with the vet the need to further protect against lyme disease, kennel cough, coronavirus and heartworms.

Regular checks for various parasites will be needed (see Chapter 30). Ears and teeth should be checked by the vet on a regular basis, even though the basic cleaning and care will be done at home.

Other than regularly scheduled visits, when should you take your Dane to the vet? Whenever you observe pain, discomfort or unusual behavior. Check frequently for lumps, bumps and cuts, and alert the vet as needed. Watch for changes in weight, eating habits, coat condition and behavior. See your vet if Rover is listless, is vomiting or has diarrhea, loses his appetite, is limping or showing signs of pain, has hair loss or skin irritations, or has an unpleasant odor such as from ears or mouth. Shallow or labored breathing warrants a vet visit, as does hiding, sweating, fever,

At least once a month, Zeus is checked for any lumps or bumps that might need veterinary attention. Black Zeus of T's Mist is owned by Michael and Mary McCracken, of Houston, Texas.

changes in urine output or appearance, straining to defecate or the appearance of blood or mucous in the feces. Of course you should also see the veterinarian if your dog is injured in any way, or shows signs of bloat (see Chapter 31).

What if there are no overt symptoms such as these, and yet you just know something is "not right?" Or perhaps your vet says all is well, but a niggling doubt remains in the back of your mind? Trust your instincts, and trust in the fact that your dog communicates with you in countless ways. Despite your veterinarian's expertise, there is no substitute for the understanding a bonded owner has for his own dog. You'll know when he's sick, even if there is no elevated temperature or other outward sign to confirm that

Some Danes are more interested in giving kisses than being checked over. Alice Haynes, of Medford, N.Y., gets kisses from one of her Pappy Jack puppies.

he's not up to par. The cost of an extra blood test is a small price to pay for your best friend's health, or just for your peace of mind.

There are excellent books on canine health available to help you gauge the severity of symptoms, communicate more efficiently with veterinary care professionals and in general take better care of your Dane.

Alternative therapies are available for dogs as well as for people, and may be of use in certain situations. Veterinary homeopathy and holistic medicine are popular as more natural ways of maintaining your dog's health. Chiropractic care has been known to help dogs who have back and neck problems or even epilepsy and skin disorders. Acupuncture can be used to treat a variety of conditions, including arthritis, skin disease and behavior problems. In the field of alternative medicine, there are reputable caregivers and there are frauds. Appendix C lists sources of further information. It is advisable to research in depth the type of therapy being considered. Don't hesitate to check with the Better Business Bureau and your local veterinary association to find out if complaints are on file. Ask for references, and make sure you are knowledgeable about and comfortable with any treatment suggested for your Dane.

IMPORTANT IMMUNIZATIONS

Rabies is a fatal viral disease which is typically transmitted by the bite of an infected animal. Rabies vaccination is not only essential, but is required by law.

Canine Distemper is a contagious viral disease that is often fatal. While puppies are more susceptible, dogs of any age should be protected from this neurological disorder. Survivors may experience damage to the central nervous system.

Canine Adenovirus Type 1 causes hepatitis, which may result in severe liver damage or death.

Canine Adenovirus Type 2 is one of the factors in infectious kennel cough. While it is impossible to protect against all components of this disease, we can immunize against three of the major factors.

Canine Bordetella is another factor in infectious kennel cough. It is particularly important to immunize your dog against kennel cough prior to an extended visit at the vet or boarding kennel.

Canine Parainfluenza is the third factor of kennel cough for which we can immunize. Vaccination is given as nose drops.

Canine Leptospirosis is a bacterial infection which can cause severe and permanent damage to the kidneys. Leptospirosis is highly contagious to both pets and people.

Canine Parvovirus is an extremely contagious disease, and is of particular danger to puppies. Parvo causes severe diarrhea and dehydration. Dogs with parvo require intensive veterinary care, fluid therapy and medications. Even with the best care, parvo can be deadly. It is much safer, easier and cheaper to protect against this disease in advance.

Canine Coronavirus is a contagious viral infection that affects the intestines, causing vomiting and diarrhea. Coronavirus is highly contagious, but not usually fatal on its own. It is sometimes seen in conjunction with parvovirus, and can make parvo even worse. Again, the preferable course of action is protection rather than treatment.

Lyme Disease is a bacterial disease that is spread through direct contact with an infected source or by insects such as flies, fleas and ticks. Beginning symptoms often mimic an arthritic condition. Lyme can be very serious for both dogs and humans.

Two faces—both radiating health and happiness. Jackson Garcia, of Pasadena, Texas, straddles Dagmar's Martina.

28

HOME HEALTH CARE

Familiarity with your dog is your best home defense against illness. If you spend quality time with Daisy, you know how she typically behaves and you'll notice unusual behavior that may signify an illness. You'll notice when she's "off her feed." You'll feel a lump or bump that wasn't there a few days ago.

It's your responsibility to protect her health with proper nutrition, good grooming and regular veterinary care. You must keep her in good physical condition with an exercise program that meets her needs, and insure both her mental and physical health with lots of social interaction and inclusion into your life and activities.

Quick response to a health problem is vital. Early treatment of an illness or injury can mean less pain for your dog, and increased opportunity for recovery. It can also mean less time and money needed to provide care. In order for the veterinarian to know about and treat your dog's illness, you must first have identified symptoms suggesting that an illness is present. Your watchful eye is your Dane's first line of defense.

Your vet will keep detailed records on Daisy's health, but an annual calendar kept at home is a real asset. Note the dates that checkups and vaccinations are due; pencil in reminders for that monthly heartworm preventive. Jot down anything that might be important; information your vet can use may be forgotten in the worry of the moment.

As mentioned in Chapter 27, you may need to know how to administer medications, take a temperature, or put a temporary bandage on an injury. You may someday need to provide first aid or emergency care designed to protect your Dane until you can reach medical help. This means you need a good emergency kit on hand.

Your emergency first-aid kit should include a good canine health and first-aid instruction book. If Daisy has any special or ongoing health problems, ask your vet to suggest relevant additions to your emergency kit.

You will need:

BLOAT KIT (See Chapter 31)
Rolls of gauze for bandaging or muzzling
Gauze squares
Nonstick wound pads
Adhesive tape
Styptic powder
Syrup of ipecac
Kaopectate
Petroleum jelly
Antibiotic ointment (from the vet)
Opthalmic ointment (from the vet)
Benadryl
Betadine
Rubbing alcohol
Hydrogen Peroxide
Activated charcoal liquid
Buffered aspirin
Pill gun for administering pills
Large syringe for administering liquids
Scissors
Tweezers
Rectal thermometer
Blanket for wrap/transport

Include in your kit phone numbers of your veterinarian, emergency clinic and poison control center. The time

Michael McCracken performs the "doggie Heimlich" on Black Zeus of T's Mist.

needed to look up these numbers or gather emergency supplies could be better spent caring for your dog's illness or injury.

Keep in mind that you also could become sick or injured some day, rendering you unable to provide basic care for Daisy. Carry information in your wallet to tell emergency personnel who to contact to care for your pet. Include information on obtaining emergency veterinary care in case your dog should be in a car accident with you.

Make sure that someone familiar to Daisy knows her needs and routine, AND IS WILLING TO CARE FOR HER IF YOU ARE INCAPACITATED. Leave written instructions with this person, other friends or family members, and your veterinarian outlining what they should do with Daisy if you are no longer able to provide care. Provisions for her ownership and care should also be spelled out in your will. Never assume that "someone" will do the right thing. The responsibility is yours!

Hopefully, your life with your Dane will be relatively carefree, with no major illnesses, accidents or emergencies. Still, while you hope for the best, prepare for the worst just in case. Always remember that this wonderful dog—your friend and companion—relies solely on you to provide the care that she cannot provide for herself. If you love her, you won't let her down.

CPR FOR DOGS

CPR (Cardiopulmonary Resuscitation) should be used in any situation that causes the heartbeat or breathing to stop or to be severely impaired. In cases of cardiac and/or respiratory arrest, you have perhaps five minutes to administer CPR. As soon as possible, get a vet on the phone to help you gauge the situation. If you have assistance, perform these emergency ministrations on the way to the nearest vet.

Artificial respiration is given by your mouth to the dog's nose. Keep in mind that a dog who is at all responsive but in shock is not himself and can be dangerous. Don't assume that your typically gentle Dane will not bite you. Shock is indicated by a rapid pulse, weakness, shallow breathing, cool paws and pale gums.

Check the mouth and nose to make sure there are no obvious obstructions. You can pull the tongue forward for a better view. If you are confident that you will not be bitten, feel around in the throat with your fingers, and pull out any obstructions you find.

IF AIRWAY IS BLOCKED AND YOU CAN'T REACH THE OBSTRUCTION: Hit against the side of the chest with your open hand four times in a row. If this does not help to eject the obstruction, perform a "doggie" version of the Heimlich maneuver. Make a fist, then grab it with the other hand. With your Dane standing, press upward into the stomach area just below the ribs four times. Check to see if the obstruction has been expelled. You can continue to repeat this sequence, giving artificial respiration if necessary after each set.

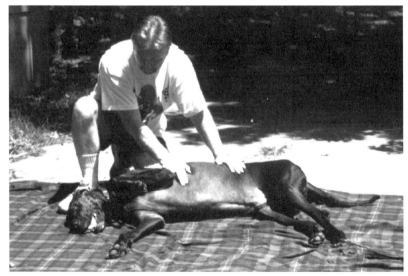

Michael McCracken checks Zeus for a heartbeat.

164

IF AIRWAY IS NOT BLOCKED BUT DOG IS UNCONSCIOUS AND NOT BREATHING: Perform mouth-to-nose artificial respiration. Pull the head and neck forward. Hold the dog's mouth closed and cover the nose completely with your mouth, using a handkerchief or cloth in between his nose and your mouth if you prefer. Exhale into the nostrils, watching to see if the chest begins to rise and fall on its own. You can continue to inflate the lungs, then allow them to deflate and check for natural breathing at least twelve times each minute. Check for a hearbeat by pressing your fingers against the lower left chest. If you can find a heartbeat, but dog is not breathing, continue respiration.

IF THERE IS NO BREATHING AND NO HEARTBEAT: Perform external cardiac compression, in conjunction with continuing artificial respiration. Place the dog on his right side on the floor. Place the heel of both your hands against the left chest just below the elbow. Allowing one or two seconds between compressions, compress the chest six times in succession. Exhale into the nostrils three times, then repeat the cycle. Continue to check for breathing and a heartbeat.

Your Dane may not regain consciousness, but you may succeed in keeping him alive until a veterinarian can take over. If he does become conscious, keep him as quiet and warm as possible while en route to emergency veterinary care. Knowing how to perform CPR may one day save the life of your Dane.

How to do a chest compression.

Hope-N-Dagon's Baron Von Bailey, owned by John Bailey, of Baytown, Texas epitomizes good health.

29

INNER WORKINGS

In order to safeguard your Dane's health, you should know the basics about the organs and functions of his body.

His skin is designed to keep out germs and protect internal organs, among other things. The health of the skin and coat can be indicative of overall health. Problems to watch for include parasites (see Chapter 30), scaling or flaking of the skin and sores or scabs.

His short coat should always be healthy looking and glossy. A dry, dull coat could be a sign of illness or nutritional deficiencies. Danes do shed, but the shedding can be controlled somewhat with good grooming practices.

Both the male and female have anal glands on each side of the rectum that secrete a foul smelling liquid which is typically expelled with bowel movements. Sometimes these glands can become impacted, leading to infection if not cleared. If Rover constantly licks or bites at his anal area or the base of his tail, the anal sacs may need to be expressed (emptied). Your vet can teach you to express the glands yourself. Ask for a demonstration. Inflammation, swelling or a foul odor are signs of infection and require veterinary care. If there are recurring problems, the veterinarian may recommend removal of the glands.

Foot pads are cushioned to act as shock absorbers. They also contain sweat glands which help to regulate body temperature. Protect Rover's foot pads against extreme cold and remember, during the summer, that concrete too hot for your bare feet is also too hot for his feet! Of course, his

The more you know about how your Dane's body functions, the better you will be able to care for her. This beautiful bitch is from Maitau Danes, owned by Patricia Ciampa and Helen Cross, Hollis, New Hampshire.

feet should also be protected from broken glass, sharp stones and lawn chemicals. Check pads frequently for signs of irritation or injury. Keep nails clipped short (see Chapter 19). Long nails can cause pain and infection, and can cause the feet to splay, or spread out. Splayed feet are more subject to irritation of the sensitive skin between the foot pads, and may cause your Dane to stand and gait improperly.

Both males and females have nipples along each side of the abdomen. In the female, the mammary glands to which these nipples are connected can produce milk for feeding her young. Changes will occur in the nipples of the Dane bitch as she ages, becomes pregnant and nurses her pups. However, since very few Great Danes should be bred at all (see Chapter 32), and most should be spayed or neutered at a young age, any lumps, bumps or changes in the nipples and surrounding area warrant veterinary attention, whether your dog is male or female. Early spaying of your female Dane can reduce the chance of uterine cancer and prevent mammary cancer.

Your dog has a belly button, which probably looks like a small scar in the center of the belly slightly down from the chest area. If your puppy has a lump in the belly button area, it may be an umbilical hernia. Usually only large umbilical hernias require treatment, but any lump should be checked by the vet to be safe.

The nose leather is fairly thick and tough. It is usually moist and cool; however, a warm, dry nose is not an indication of a fever! If Rover appears to be under the weather, use a thermometer to gauge his temperature and consult your veterinarian if it is over 102.5 degrees. Your vet will be happy to give you a lesson in proper temperature taking.

Rover has whiskers over his eyes, and on his face, chin and muzzle. The whiskers act as sensory organs and may help him to better orient himself in poor light. Danes shown in conformation typically have their whiskers clipped close in order to better show off the face and muzzle.

There are over 300 bones in your Great Dane's body. The bones store certain minerals until needed, and form the skeleton to protect internal organs. Bone marrow stores fat and is instrumental in the formation of red blood cells and antibodies. Joints attach certain bones to each other and provide range of movement. Bone and joint problems in Danes are usually the result of genetic disorders passed down by ancestors, or of poor nutrition and/or too much exercise during growth periods. Many problems of this nature can be avoided by buying only from breeders who test breeding stock for genetic defects such as hip dysplasia. Read carefully the chapters on Exercise (Chapter 18) and Nutrition (Chapter 20); don't hesitate to seek advice from your veterinarian or breeder. Immediately advise your vet if you notice signs of lameness or discomfort of movement, especially during puppyhood and adolescence.

Muscles give your dog power for moving, digestion, blood circulation and other functions. Simple muscle strain is usually handled with enforced rest and possibly buffered aspirin to reduce discomfort. Any serious strain or muscle problem, or even a simple strain continuing more than a couple of days, warrants veterinary diagnosis. Remember that your vet is always the best person to judge the seriousness of an injury or illness.

The heart itself is a muscle which contracts independently to pump blood. The heart is part of the cardiovascular system, along with the arteries and veins, which carry the blood, and the spleen, which performs several blood-related functions. Complete blood counts are often done on sick dogs so that the illness can be diagnosed and treated properly. Dogs have blood types just as people do. You can ask your veterinarian to type your Dane's blood in advance of illnesses; this would save time in an emergency. The normal heartbeat of a Great Dane is approximately 80 to 90 beats a minute when at rest. Heart disease can be signalled by many symptoms, including difficulty in breathing, persistent coughing and progressive lethargy. See your veterinarian immediately if Rover exhibits any of these symptoms. Congenital heart disease does show up in Great Danes—just one more reason to deal with a reliable breeder who tests breeding stock for genetic defects. Heartworms, which are transmitted by mosquitoes, can be avoided by keeping your Dane on heartworm preventive medication according to your veterinarian's instructions. The symptoms of heartworm disease are much the same as those of other cardiac diseases.

Your dog's eyes are similar to yours in many ways, but there are important differences. His eyes are more sensitive to movement, yet he cannot see detail to the extent a human can. The dog has better night vision, but cannot see as well in bright light as his companion person. His color vision is limited. Dogs have a third eyelid which people do not have. The third eyelid is a membrane between the eye and the outer eyelid. This nictating membrane is very noticeable in many Danes, and is not a cause for alarm. However, any irritation to the eye or differences in the appear-

Black Zeus of T's Mist, owned by the author, has a healthy, glossy coat.

ance of the eye should be checked by a veterinarian. The eyes are very delicate and easily damaged. Also, many serious diseases show up initially in eye changes or inflammation.

The visible part of Rover's ear is called the pinna. It is made of cartilage and is designed to direct sound vibrations to the eardrum, which is in the middle part of the ear. The inner ear contains nerves that transmit the sound to the brain, and serves as the balance center. Signs of ear parasites or infection include scratching at the ear, persistent head shaking, irritation, large amounts of ear wax accumulation, and foul smelling secretions. If Rover cries or pulls away when his ears are touched, have them checked for infection. The outer portions of the ear can be cleaned with gauze and mineral oil; never attempt to poke anything into the ear canal.

The process of food digestion begins in the mouth. The teeth are designed to cut and tear food; they also serve as weapons when needed. The adult dog should have 42 teeth. The gums should be firm and pink; the teeth should be firm with no excessive stains or tartar. Any bleeding or swelling in the mouth should be examined by the veterinarian. Be sure to inspect the mouth and brush the teeth regularly (see Chapter 19).

Food passes through the esophagus into the stomach, where food breakdown begins. The small intestine does most of the actual digestive work, absorbing water, electrolytes and nutrients. The pancreas secretes enzymes which help in digestion and stimulate the gall bladder to produce bile, also helpful in the digestive process. The large intestine absorbs any water and nutrients remaining. Waste material is then passed through the anus. From ingestion

Rolls shows tremendous muscle power! This powerful Dane is Am. & Can. Ch. & Can. O.T. Ch. Danehaven's Rolling Thunder UDT, Can. UDTDX, WDX, HC, U-CDX, TDI owned by Marta Brock, Rolling Thunder Danes, Olympia, Washington.

of food to passage of wastes usually takes about two days.

The pancreas and the liver are also parts of the digestive system. The pancreas regulates glucose and provides digestive enzymes to the small intestine. The liver is extremely important for producing bile to aid in absorbing fat, for metabolizing carbohydrates and proteins, and for detoxifying digestive byproducts. The liver is also instrumental in the blood clotting function. Most digestive problems are signalled by vomiting and/or diarrhea. Loss of weight and appetite are symptomatic of gastrointestinal disease.

The respiratory tract, beginning at the nose, carries air through the windpipe and various bronchial tubes to the lungs where oxygen and carbon dioxide are exchanged. The nose also works with the olfactory nerves to provide a highly developed sense of smell. Any unusual secretions from the nose should be checked by the veterinarian; normal secretion is clear, watery and not excessive. Air travelling across and vibrating the vocal cords on its way to the lungs enables the dog to produce sounds. Each part of the respiratory tract can become infected or diseased. Breathing difficulties or abnormalities, coughing, sneezing and hoarseness are signs of respiratory distress.

The endocrine system consists of a number of glands that manufacture hormones and release them into the blood. Endocrine glands include the pituitary, pancreas and thyroid, among others. Skin problems and hair loss can be indicative of an endocrine problem, but there are varying symptoms of the different disorders. Hypothyroidism and diabetes are only two of many endocrine diseases. Diagnosis is usually based on symptoms and blood work. Most endocrine system disfunctions are very treatable.

Your Dane has hundreds of lymph nodes throughout his body. The lymph nodes produce special cells that regulate the immune system. Failures in the immune system can affect virtually any part of the body.

The nervous system includes the brain, spinal cord, and the peripheral and cranial nerves. The brain is the center of all reasoning and behavior, including sight, hearing, and the instinct to survive. The spinal cord enables Rover to interpret sensation in his limbs. Nerves send messages to the muscles. Disease or injury can affect the nervous system in any number of ways, including gait and movement difficulties or abnormalities, seizures, vision loss, paralysis and coma. Epilepsy is one example of a nervous system disorder.

The kidneys filter toxins and waste materials in the blood stream, concentrating these wastes into urine which is stored in the bladder until urination. Urinary tract problems, including incontinence, infections and bladder stones, are common in dogs. Inform your vet if your Dane has changes in urine color, blood in the urine, difficulty in urinating, or is incontinent.

The testicles of your male Dane should drop from the abdomen into the scrotum by six or eight weeks of age. If one or both testicles fails to drop, it is best to have the dog neutered to avoid the increased likelihood of testicular cancer. A dog with undescended testicles cannot be shown in conformation.

The penis is contained within a skin covering called a sheath. The penis itself is typically pink. Any secretions from the penis of your puppy should be clear; as he matures, you may notice a slight yellowish, cloudy discharge.

The reproductive system of the female is mostly internal, including the uterus and ovaries. Any secretion from the vaginal area should be slight and clear, unless your bitch is in heat. Spaying your female will prevent both the heat cycle and pregnancy, and will greatly benefit the health of your female by reducing the chance of mammary cancer and eliminating the chance of both uterine cancer and pyometra.

If you are considering breeding your Dane, male or female, a complete physical and urogenital exam should be done to rule out diseases, infections and structural deformities.

30

PARASITES

Fleas, ticks, worms, mites—all dog owners deal with one or more parasites during the life of their dog. And while the information in this chapter cannot replace a good canine home health care manual, and certainly not your veterinarian, it can help you to know what to watch for and what initial steps to take.

There are a number of worms that can affect your dog. Your veterinarian will check for various types during routine physical exams, which is one good reason for having those semi-annual or annual checkups, even though Daisy seems just fine. Between these scheduled visits, alert your vet if you suspect an infestation of worms or other parasites.

Puppies with thin bodies and pot bellies are likely to have roundworms. They can cause diarrhea, and are often vomited up by the puppy. They are dangerous, both to your dog and to you. Luckily, they are not difficult to eradicate.

Hookworms can be deadly, especially for young puppies. Bloody diarrhea and pale gums may suggest hookworms. Your veterinarian can provide effective care if caught in a reasonable time.

Tapeworms can usually be seen on your dog's stool. A weekly glance at Daisy's droppings can show evidence of tapeworms, as well as diarrhea, blood in the stool, and other problems. Tapeworms are carried by fleas and easily transmitted from dog to dog. Your vet will probably suggest better flea control, in addition to a deworming agent, if tapeworm infestation is frequent.

Whipworms are indicated by weight loss, anemia and watery or bloody diarrhea. They are dangerous, particularly in older dogs, and can even necessitate emergency surgery in some cases.

Heartworms are transmitted through the bite of mosquitoes. They lodge in the heart and may eventually cause death if not treated. Even the treatment itself can be dangerous. However, heartworm can be prevented. Talk to your vet about daily or monthly preventive medication. Daisy will need a blood test to determine that she's heartworm-negative before beginning the medication, and will need to be tested annually thereafter.

There are also microscopic parasites that can affect dogs, particularly during puppyhood. These include coccidiosis, giardia, trichomonas, and intestinal flukes. Per-

A trip to the vet need not be traumatic. Ch. Maitau's Designated Driver CC enjoys the outing. Owned by Patricia Ciampa and Helen Cross, Maitau Danes, Hollis, New Hampshire.

sistent diarrhea and re-
lated problems are indi-
cators of a possible proto-
zoan infestation.

Mites are usually
found in the ear, and are
easily passed from dog to
dog. Symptoms of ear
mites include head shak-
ing, scratching at the ears,
and smelly debris in the
ears. Ear mites are typi-
cally treated with clean-
ing and prescription
medication. Mange is also

14-month old Brees' Pinky Leigh is
in beautiful condition. This lovely
pointed bitch is owned by Debbie
Cole, Brees' Danes, Garland, Texas.

caused by a mite, is highly infectious and can be miserable
for your dog. Early diagnosis is very helpful in treating
mange.

If both your Dane and her living quarters are kept
reasonably clean, you will probably never have a problem
with lice. However, it is possible for Daisy to contract lice
from coming in contact with an infested animal. A dog with
lice experiences constant itching. The nits are large enough
to be seen easily. Common flea preparations can rid your
dog of lice; disinfect bedding and living areas as well.

Examine Daisy for ticks during routine grooming
sessions, especially if she has been in tall grasses or wooded
areas. The female tick swells from the ingestion of your
dog's blood. The smaller male does not eat blood meals,
but may be found close to the female. Your dog may need
to be seen by a vet for a serious tick invasion, but one or
two can be easily removed at home. Use flea spray to make
the tick let go, then remove it with tweezers and flush it
down the toilet. Ticks carry many diseases that can be dangerous to your dog and to you, including lyme disease,
Rocky Mountain spotted fever and St. Louis encephalitis.

Many people believe that, when you have a dog,
fleas simply go with the territory. It is not "normal," nor is

it okay, to force Daisy to live with a flea infestation. Even a few fleas can cause such problems as tapeworms and skin allergies. And unfortunately, those few fleas will quickly turn into many, making both of you miserable. The more fleas attacking your dog, the more blood loss she will suffer. She could become ill or even die, particularly if she is very young, geriatric, weakened from another illness, or allergic to flea bites.

There are thousands of flea control products on the market; use only those approved by your veterinarian as safe. Many vets now prescribe a monthly flea-control pill, actually a flea development inhibitor, which can be given to your dog at the same time as his heartworm preventive. Regardless of the flea fighting method you choose, follow directions exactly, and remember—to eradicate fleas from your home you must treat your dog's surroundings as well as the dog itself. Treat all pets at the same time as you treat the house and yard. If you hire an exterminator, make sure he or she knows about the pets in your home.

There are no short cuts to ridding your Dane and your home of fleas, but it can be done. In between flea control treatments, vacuum your home frequently and make sure to discard the vacuum bag. If the bag is left in your home, flea eggs that were sucked up will hatch in the bag and attack your dog and your home all over again!

There are many natural herbs and oils believed to repel fleas. Natural methods are probably more useful in preventing a flea problem than in eliminating an already present infestation. Again, make sure your veterinarian has approved your flea control methods as safe and effective.

31

A WORD ABOUT BLOAT

BLOAT IS A LIFE THREATENING EMERGENCY. Familiarize yourself with the symptoms, and seek immediate veterinary care if your Dane experiences them.

Officially called Gastric Dilatation/Torsion Complex, bloat occurs when the stomach fills up with gas and swells very large. As the stomach swells, pressure is placed upon other internal organs. The first signs of bloat are excessive salivation, nausea and repeated, often unsuccessful, attempts to vomit; the swelling then becomes evident. As the diaphragm becomes hampered by the swelling, the dog experiences difficulty in breathing. Pressure on veins prevents blood from being returned to the heart and the dog goes into shock, becoming confused and weak with pale mucous membranes and a rapid heartbeat. If not treated rapidly, the dog will collapse and die. Treatment often includes emergency surgery.

Veterinarians are not sure exactly what causes bloat, but it is a severe problem in the Great Dane and other large breeds. There are ways to reduce the chances of your Dane experiencing bloat. Be very consistent about what and when your dog eats. Don't change her diet unless it is absolutely necessary. Make any necessary changes slowly by adding a small amount of the new food to the old, and gradually increasing the amount of the new while reducing the amount of the old. This should be done over several days. Many people will advise you to soak dry food in water before feeding to help prevent bloat. This is probably an outdated notion because today's quality dry foods are meat-based rather than cereal-based, meaning there is no soy or other fast fermenting grain to foam and swell in the stomach. Soaking the food may even cause a loss of essential nutrients.

While treats can and should be used for training, don't overdo. Great Danes do not require huge treats simply because they are big dogs; use small treats as rewards. Don't get into the habit of dishing out a handful of treats each time your dog seems to want them; offer attention and play instead.

Feed two or three small meals each day. Don't allow exercise or heavy water consumption for an hour before and one to two hours after meals. Avoid situations that would encourage your Dane to gulp her food, such as having to compete with other dogs at mealtime. If you are detained away from home and your dog misses a meal, do not overfeed to compensate. Remember that stress, such as loud and physical family arguments, may be a contributing factor to bloat.

Never leave your Dane after feeding. She should be observed for an hour or two after meals. If she bloated while you were gone, she could easily be beyond help by the time you returned. If you suspect bloat, a quick reaction may save your dog's life. Seek veterinary help **IMMEDIATELY**. If you cannot reach a vet within 20 minutes, you may wish to consider performing emergency treatment at home. This means you should assemble a "bloat kit" and **talk through all the necessary steps in advance with your veterinarian**. Even if you are sure you know what to do, it would be best to contact your vet by telephone and have her walk you through the actual procedure.

Your bloat kit should include:

- a large bore stomach tube (should be measured in advance to the length of the 10th rib of your Dane—

Giant breeds, like the Dane, are prone to bloat. This is Rojon's Famous Amos, an impressive pointed male bred by Ray Cataldi and owned by Carol Beene, Crickhollow Danes, Denton, Texas. He is handled by Michael Chiles.

ask your vet for the tube and for assistance in determining the exact length), an oral speculum (obtainable from your vet or a veterinary supply; you can also use a 1" x 10 yd. roll of electrician's tape if necessary—make sure in advance that the tube fits through the hole in the center of the roll), a 1 1/2" length needle, 14 gauge or larger

- a gas absorbent (Digel or other* as recommended by your vet)
- Novalsan solution
- KY jelly
- a list of emergency instructions, phone number of the vet and/or emergency clinic, and a note reminding you of your dog's regular pulse rate when healthy (ask your vet to demonstrate taking the pulse)

*(Many breeders recommend, in place of Digel, a cup of grapefruit juice followed by 2-4 tablespoons of probiotic and digestive enzyme powder mixed in cool water—Sources are noted in Appendix C)

You should review the emergency procedure step by step with your veterinarian as soon as possible after obtaining your Dane. If your dog is symptomatic, and you have determined that you cannot reach veterinary care in a reasonable amount of time, you will need to tube the dog.

You should never leave your Dane unattended after eating. This is pointed CloudNines Barkley Sir Charles CGC, TDI, owned by Loleta and Doug Turner, Eureka, California.

The oral speculum is placed in the dog's mouth just behind the front teeth. The hole should be placed in the direction of the head and tail, NOT the cheeks. Wind a strip of tape around the muzzle to keep the speculum in its proper place. Coat the tube with the KY jelly, except for a small strip at the very end of the tube for you to hold. Use a gentle twist to move the tube into the stomach. If the tube will not go down, do not force. Pull it out and try again. When the tube reaches the stomach, you will both hear and smell the subsequent release of gas, and the stomach will begin to appear smaller. You may need to administer Digel or a substitute (see above) through the tube to break up excess foam and help the stomach to go down. When the stomach seems to be empty, stand behind the dog, facing the same direction as the dog, lean over and grasp around the abdomen with locked wrists and squeeze to remove as much of the remaining stomach contents as possible. If tubing is unsuccessful, there is a last resort emergency procedure called percutaneous trocharization. Use the novalsan solution to prepare the area just behind the last rib. Remove the cap of the needle, grasp the needle's blunt end and sharply stab into the left side, immediately behind the last rib. If you get blood in the needle, you have hit the spleen and must try again. When you successfully pierce the stomach, it will distend, hopefully making it possible for you to tube the dog.

The successful use of this emergency procedure **DOES NOT** negate the necessity of seeking veterinary help. Your dog may still require surgery to attach the stomach to the abdominal wall to prevent future twisting, or at least need an IV solution to combat shock. Also, the shock experienced by the dog can cause severe heart abnormalities and other potentially life threatening problems. When your emergency ministrations have been completed, transport your Dane to the nearest veterinarian **IMMEDIATELY**.

Though the causes of bloat are still relatively unknown, there have been recent improvements in drug therapy, surgical techniques and aftercare. We can only hope that research will soon provide us with better information on preventing this terrible condition altogether.

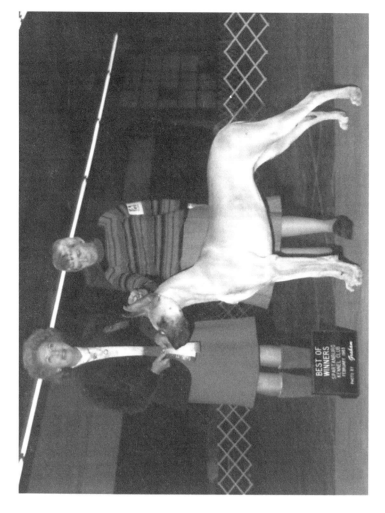

Championship status can be an indicator of breeding quality. This 10-month-old bitch became Ch. Von Shrado's Easter Bonnet. She is owned by Sandy and Jim Hann, Von Shrado Danes, Pikeville, N.C.

32

SHOULD YOU BREED YOUR GREAT DANE?

The answer to that question is almost always NO! Very few dogs of any breed have all of the necessary characteristics for good breeding stock. Before you even entertain the thought of breeding, ask yourself a few questions about your dog's suitability for producing offspring:

1) Is your Dane registered with the AKC and/or UKC?
2) Is your dog from a breeding planned and overseen by a reputable, responsible breeder and NOT a backyard breeder or a puppy mill (See Chapter 8), or from an "accidental," unplanned and possibly unsuitable mating?
3) As you look over your dog's pedigree, particularly the last three generations, do you see several titled dogs? Whether they are conformation champions or are titled in obedience, tracking, etc., is it obvious that your Dane's ancestors were fine, healthy, capable specimens of the breed?
4) Does your Great Dane have a really good temperament—stable and friendly—and high intelligence?
5) Is your dog a breed champion, or pointed toward championship status? If not, does he or she at least closely fit the breed standard and have other titles demonstrating talent or intelligence?
6) Has your dog been tested and certified free of genetic diseases such as hip dysplasia? And has your

veterinarian found your Dane to be sound and healthy in every way?

If you have answered "no" to even ONE of these questions, please do the responsible thing and have your Dane spayed or neutered. Even if you were able to honestly answer "yes" to all six questions, there are still good reasons NOT to breed.

Consider the health risks and possible costs to your dog. Intact males are more likely to suffer prostatic disease and testicular cancer. At the very least, they suffer from severe sexual frustration—possibly even psychological damage—when not being bred. Intact males are more likely to roam in search of a female in heat, and more likely to mark your home with urine. They are also more aggressive, less social, and harder to housebreak, train and control.

Intact females are more likely to suffer uterine cancer, mammary cancer and pyometra. Heat periods are uncomfortable for her and messy for you. Male dogs may come from miles around to camp on your doorstep. They are likely to be aggressive toward each other while in pursuit of your bitch, and may even be aggressive toward you. They will mark your property, leave messes in your yard, make noise, and make it almost impossible to take your dog out of the house for a walk or a potty break.

Pregnancy itself is not without risk. Hemorrhaging, spontaneous abortion, ectopic pregnancy and other very serious situations can arise. Problems at delivery time can also put your Dane's life at risk, along with the lives of her pups.

Both males and females can have structural abnormalities or infertility problems that make mating difficult, painful, impossible, or simply useless. Dogs, like people, may have sexually transmitted diseases that can be passed on during the mating process.

Consider the financial ramifications. If you are the owner of the male, you're probably looking forward to that

Many choose a champion sire, like Alice Haynes' Ch. Pappy Jack's Justin Time, who makes his home in Medford, New York. *(DiGiacomo photo)*

stud fee, thinking perhaps that this is an easy way to make money. Offset that stud fee by the costs of a complete physical exam, x-rays and blood work to rule out genetic disorders, and other health and fitness checks to be sure your dog is sound and breedable. You may be surprised at how small (or even nonexistent) that stud fee will become!

If you own the bitch, you will most likely have to pay a stud fee or give up the pick of the litter to the owner of the male. You must insure the health and genetic soundness of the bitch prior to breeding. You will spend quite a bit of money for an overall physical exam, x-rays and bloodwork. If she has trouble mating or is infertile, there will be additional costs to identify and repair the problem, if indeed it can be repaired.

Regular veterinary care is essential during pregnancy; should an emergency arise, costs can skyrocket! If there are delivery problems, you may be facing a bill for a

187

It's expensive and time consuming to care for a litter. Dagmar's Martina nurses her pups at Penny and Rich Garcia's home in Pasadena, Texas.

Caesarean section. All this, and you haven't even begun to care for the pups! Proper nutrition, health checks, worming, immunizations, ear cropping—the list goes on and on. Did you plan to breed in order to make money? You're much more likely to spend, spend, spend!

Still want to breed your dog? Think about your long-term responsibility. Are you prepared to find proper homes for a dozen puppies? Until you find those homes, can you provide food, medical care, grooming, training and attention to each and every one? Can you afford to keep any for whom homes are not available? Can you offer a health guarantee on these puppies, knowing that you bred responsibly for good health and temperament and the betterment of the breed? Are you prepared to take back puppies who fall under that health guarantee, or simply don't work out in their new homes?

Those puppies will be in this world because you decided they should be born. You are responsible for their health and welfare. If one of the puppies you breed ends up in an animal shelter because of behavior problems, or wracks up thousands of dollars in vet bills for an inherited health problem, you are responsible.

It's a tall order—one best left to professionals. Don't make your dog and his or her puppies suffer because you didn't know what you were getting into. If you breed, you can certainly hope and pray that everything goes right— but you must be prepared to deal with the consequences should everything go wrong.

Breeders should be those few hearty souls who understand the breed standard backward and forward, and know exactly how their dogs compare. They must know the principles of genetics and heredity, and be proficient in matching dogs that will complement each other's strengths and weaknesses, and produce excellent puppies. Breeders should hold a reputable place in the dog world and the Great Dane fancy, knowing inside and out the needs and requirements of their breed. They must be willing and able to be responsible for the health and happiness of the dogs they own and the dogs they breed.

The breeder's world is one of dog shows and championship points, toplines and gaits, club meetings, vet visits, grooming sessions, rescue missions, obedience classes, breeding seminars, pedigrees, and yes, lots of love and pride—hopefully even some recognition. It is also a world of high costs, tremendous commitment, and sometimes heartbreak. Maybe you are one of those very few who have the time, the money, the willingness to work very hard, the background and the knowledge to be a good breeder.

One-week-old Dagmar's Blaze will grow quickly. Owned by Penny and Rick Garcia, Dagmar Danes.

If you are, do your homework, make your decisions carefully and wisely, and breed good dogs that will be healthy, happy family companions for caring people.

But if what you really are is a Great Dane lover who wants to raise another puppy, contact a breeder with the aforementioned qualifications and buy one. Maybe you want one "just like Daisy." Call up Daisy's breeder and tell him what you're looking for.

Maybe you just like the idea of having more Danes around the house. Terrific! Don't add to an already huge pet overpopulation problem—call up a Dane rescue group (See Chapter 14) and provide a home for one or more Danes who are waiting for a loving, responsible family. Then give yourself a big pat on the back and enjoy your spayed or neutered, truly GREAT Great Dane(s)—after all, you've proven you deserve the best!

SECTION IV

ACTIVITIES FOR YOU
AND YOUR DANE

The height of show ring success! Multiple Best in Show winner Ch. Aquino's Little Dooz Coupe SDS was the nation's top Dane. This magnificent male is owned by Beverly Hauer, Hauerdane, Alpine, California.

33

CONFORMATION— SHOWING YOUR DANE

The breed ring is the canine equivalent of a beauty contest. Your dog will be judged on his looks and style, based on how he conforms to the breed standard of excellence (See Appendix A).

If you have purchased a show quality puppy, it is extremely important that you socialize him very well. He must become accustomed to being in crowds, with lots of people and lots of dogs. He must not object to being handled, including having his bite checked.

As soon as your puppy's immunizations are complete, take him out and introduce him to the world! Teach him to enjoy car rides and meeting new people and dogs by giving him lots of attention and praise. Find a good training club where other members are showing in conformation. This is the easiest way to learn to show off your Dane to his best advantage. Instructors and other club members will show you how to prepare yourself and your dog for a show, how to "stack" the dog for the judge's examination, when to "bait" him with treats and how to call attention to his best attributes. The best conformation-handling classes are often taught by all-breed handlers who know just how a dog should be presented.

Many people prefer to hire a professional handler to take their dog into the ring. You gain the advantage of experience and even "trade secrets" when a professional presents your dog. Some judges will not seriously consider

Young puppies are trained to "stack." Sweet Pea was a beautiful puppy who grew up to be a champion. She is owned by Beverly Hauer, Hauerdane, Alpine, California.

dogs being handled by amateurs.

If you choose to hire a handler, look for someone who has shown Great Danes in the past. You want someone who obviously likes Rover, and that both of you feel comfortable with. Make sure you ask lots of questions before choosing a handler. Does she take care of show entries? What are the fees and how does the billing work? Who will handle grooming? What happens if showing your dog conflicts with showing another client's dog? Remember, you're going to have to pay the handler's fee even when Rover loses, and it can get expensive. Make sure you know what to expect for your money.

Perhaps you can't afford a professional handler, or would simply like to be in the spotlight yourself. It may be harder for an amateur to campaign a dog, but it can be done successfully. The main thing you need is a good quality dog with lots of pizazz and showmanship. A good tempered dog with lots of style and a "look at me" attitude can often make up for faults in the dog and handler errors.

Remember that this is a learning experience. Plan to have a good time with Rover, and be patient! You may have quite a few shows under your belt before those ribbons start rolling in!

Some fellow competitors will give you helpful advice; others may be downright rude. Take it in stride, take pride in your dog and keep your confidence up. Those people with their noses in the air were once beginners just like you! Remember to keep your Dane perfectly groomed and in top-notch physical condition. Give him lots of praise for his efforts, successful or not. After all, you could be the reason he hasn't won yet! Laugh at your own mistakes and his, and learn from them. Sooner or later you'll both know what you're doing.

When you venture into the ring, it's best to start at match shows. You won't earn any points toward a championship, but you'll have a chance to learn the ropes at a relatively low cost. Judges at match shows will often give you advice on presenting your dog. When you move up to AKC point shows, expect increased expense and competition, but you'll then be working toward that coveted championship. Your Dane will compete against other Great Danes of the same sex. There are six classes for each sex. Puppy classes are for dogs between six months and one year of age. There is also a Twelve to Eighteen Month class. Novice is for dogs who have not yet won a first prize. Bred by Exhibitor is for any dog over six months who is not a champion, and is owned and shown by a person or kennel representative who is recognized as the dog's breeder on AKC records. The American-bred class is for dogs born in the United States. Open is for all dogs, American and foreign bred.

Winners of these classes move up to Winners competition, where two ribbons are awarded

This four-month old pup aleady has a "look at me" attitude. Hauerdane's Plain in the Dark is owned by Beverly Hauer, Hauerdane, Alpine, California.

for Winners and Reserve Winners. These two dogs go into competition for Best Of Breed, along with dogs of either sex who are already champions. The Best of Breed Dane goes on to compete in Working Group competition against the best of the other breeds in the group. The Winners male and Winners bitch compete for the honor of Best of Winners. Should a Dane be chosen Best of Working Group, he or she would then compete for Best of Show. The dog chosen Best of Show is the one dog left undefeated at the end of the show's final competition.

Points are awarded on the basis of the number of dogs competing. Only the Winners dog and Winners bitch receive championship points. A major is any show in which three or more points is awarded to a winning dog. To become a champion, your dog must earn fifteen points with at least two wins at major shows under two different judges.

UKC conformation is beginning to catch on with dog fanciers. Your UKC registered Dane can earn the title of UKC Show Champion (CH.) by winning a minimum of 100 points. Points must be earned under at least three different judges. Wins must include at least two Best Male or Female under two different judges. The UKC Grand Show Champion (GR. CH.) designation is earned by winning five Champion of Champions show classes. Wins must take place in at least five different UKC shows under at least three different judges. Complete Rules and Regulations are available from the UKC. (See Appendix C)

If your puppy with show potential grows to be an adult with none, it just means that conformation is not the activity for this particular dog. Perhaps he's meant to be a flyball champion, capture a tracking title or receive recognition as an obedience Utility Dog. He's definitely meant to be your loving companion and best friend!

34

THE CANINE GOOD CITIZEN PROGRAM

Your Great Dane should be raised and trained to be a good citizen. Why not go a step further and let Daisy strut her stuff and place a CGC after her name to denote her accomplishment?

The Canine Good Citizen Companionship Program is an AKC program designed to insure that your dog knows—and minds—her manners. The CGC recognizes your dog for her good behavior, and you for responsible pet ownership. To participate in the test, you must show proof that Daisy has a valid rabies vaccination and is licensed according to the requirements in your community.

To pass the test, Daisy must demonstrate her ability to meet certain requirements. She must walk calmly on a leash and not pull. She must show that she is well-behaved when she is greeted by a stranger, petted and groomed. She will be required to show her comprehension of the commands "sit," "down" and "stay." She must stay calm around everyday distractions such as groups of people, joggers and other dogs. She will be supervised to see if she can stay put and show good behavior when you are out of her sight. Meeting these requirements will demonstrate that your dog knows how to behave in public, and that she is a calm and trustworthy companion.

Contact the AKC for complete information and a list of testing sites and dates. There may be training clubs in your area that can help you and your Dane in preparing for the test. Many clubs administer the tests in conjunction with obedience and conformation trials. If you have other dogs in the house—including mixed breeds—make sure they participate in the program also. Every dog can become a Canine Good Citizen!

Hope-N-Dagon's Baron Von Bailey is well-behaved when greeted by a stranger.

35

OBEDIENCE COMPETITION

A beginning obedience class is the perfect place for your Dane to learn the basic commands she needs to know to be safe, secure and well-behaved. If you discover that the two of you enjoy working and learning together, consider going on to compete in the obedience ring. Working with an obedience training club will give you an edge, but if there isn't one nearby, take advantage of the numerous books available on obedience training and competition.

Keep in mind that long practices and forced exercise are unacceptable for the Dane puppy. Train in very short sessions, at least until adolescence. Even then, have your vet do a physical exam before beginning competitive obedience. Competing in Open, where your dog will be required to jump over obstacles, is best left for adulthood in order to protect growing bones and joints.

AKC Obedience competition starts with Novice classes. If this is your first obedience dog, you will compete in Novice A. If you have previously handled a dog with a CD in the obedience ring, you must compete in Novice B. A CD, or Companion Dog title, will be bestowed on your Dane when she achieves three scores of 170 or more points out of a possible 200 under three different judges. To do this, she must be proficient at a number of exercises, including proper heeling on leash and in a figure 8 pattern (worth 40 possible points), standing for examination by the judge (30 possible points), heeling free (40 possible points),

Many Danes love obedience competition. Can. Ch. Paquestone's V. Rolling Thunder CDX, TD, Can. CDX, TD, U-CD, ASCA-CD, WD, TDI takes the bar jump with style. Owned by Marta Brock, Rolling Thunder Danes, Olympia, Washington.

the recall, which means staying where left and responding quickly when called (30 possible points), remaining in a sit/stay for one minute (30 possible points) and a down/stay for three minutes (30 possible points). It's not as easy as it sounds!

Once your dog has her CD, the two of you can compete in Open classes. Again, three scores of 170 or more under three different judges are needed to earn a title, in this case a CDX or Companion Dog Excellent. The exercises in Open include heeling free and the figure 8 (40 possible points), drop on recall (30 possible points), retrieving a dumbbell on a flat surface (20 possible points), retrieving the dumbbell over a high jump (30 possible points) and a broad jump (20 possible points), remaining in a sit/stay for three minutes (30 possible points) and a down/stay for five minutes (30 possible points), both with you out of sight.

You can continue to compete in Open no matter what obedience titles your dog holds, but once she has that CDX, you'll compete in Open B. Your CDX dog can compete in Utility A or B, with B including UD (Utility Dog title) dogs. Exercises in Utility include the signal exercise in which you and your dog demonstrate teamwork and the ability of your dog to respond properly to hand signals (40 possible points), and scent discrimination in which your dog must select an article with your scent from among other articles (2 separate exercises worth a possible 30 points each). There is also a directed retrieve exercise in which your dog must retrieve the correct one of three gloves according to your hand signal (30 possible points), a moving stand for examination in which you have your dog heel, then stand/stay while you walk away and while the judge examines her, then come when you call and sit in a heel position (30 possible points). The last Utility exercise is directed jumping, in which your dog must respond correctly to a hand signal directing her to jump over either a high jump or a bar jump (40 possible points).

Susan Barney teaches Hotshot, better known as Nightwatch Fire N Ice V. Hogcreek, how to take the dumbbell.

UD titled dogs can earn points toward an Obedience Trial Championship (OT Ch). Dogs must win 100 points, including a first place

in Utility or Utility B with at least three dogs in competition, a first place in Open B with at least six dogs competing, and another first place in either class. The three first places wins must be under three different judges.

There is also a relatively new AKC obedience title, the Utility Dog Excellent (UDX). Your Dane can earn a UDX by qualifying in both Open B and Utility B at ten obedience trials. It is possible for Rover to obtain his UDX without being an OTCh.

Show offs! Marta Brock's "Bumper" takes the jump, while "Rolls" holds the upright. Rolling Thunder Danes.

It is equally possible to become an OTCh without holding the UDX. There are non-regular obedience clases for special dogs, such as Veterans for dogs eight years of age and older, and Versatility for dogs who know all the exercises in Novice through Utility.

The UKC also offers obedience trials and titles. The U-CD can be earned by dogs in Novice A or B. The dog must receive three qualifying scores of at least 170 points at three different trials under two different judges. At least 50% of possible points must be earned in each exercise. The requirements are the same for earning a U-CDX in Open A or B, and a U-UD in Utility A or B. Actual exercises to be performed are slightly different than those required in AKC competition. A complete Rules and Regulations book can be obtained from the United Kennel Club (Appendix C).

No matter how far you go in the sport, you'll find that obedience is a great hobby and increases the bond you have with your Dane.

36

THE GREAT DANE AS THERAPY DOG

If you'd like to spend time with your Dane while providing a much-needed service to your community, consider volunteer work with an animal-assisted therapy organization.

Your Dane needn't be a star athlete for this activity, but he must be clean, parasite-free, extremely well-behaved and comfortable in meeting the public. He should be somewhat outgoing, yet stable and calm. He must certainly be trained not to be pushy or to jump on people. A good therapy dog is not alarmed by wheelchairs, walkers and other medical equipment. He is not bothered by crowded elevators. (Caution: While many Danes need to be comfortable in an elevator, you should always enter and exit very carefully! If the doors should close with you on one side and your leashed Dane on the other, Rover could be seriously injured or killed.) Most of all, your dog should enjoy lots of hugs and attention! Many obedience clubs have a therapy group, or you can contact the organizations listed in Appendix C.

Therapy groups are designed to provide positive interaction with animals, often for those who are institutionalized and unable to keep a companion animal. In addition to visiting nursing homes and hospitals, some groups offer education sessions in schools and at community events.

It has been proven that interacting with animals reduces stress and helps people to feel better about

Walhalla's Liebestraum CD, CGC and Siegreich's Amstel V. Nahallac CDX, CGC visit a patient. These harlequins are owned by Chris and Henry Bredenkamp, Siegreich Danes, Burleson, Texas.

themselves. Many think that animals can even transfer their own energy to those in need. Numerous breakthroughs in patients' physical and mental health have been made thanks to the unconditional love and acceptance provided by a dog or cat.

You will probably be required to attend a workshop or two to prepare you and Rover for dealing with people who may be physically or mentally ill, or disabled in some way. Temperament testing will no doubt be done to insure that your dog is calm, friendly and mannerly in a variety of situations.

A visit from your dog can be the highlight of someone's week or month, and may even improve their long-term health and well-being. Your Dane will enjoy being the center of attention, and you'll feel wonderful for the gifts of love, hope and laughter that you and Rover have given to those in need.

37

COMPETITION, EXERCISE AND JUST PLAIN FUN!

Your Great Dane needs both physical and mental activity in order to be healthy and happy. Participating together in games and fun events will increase the bond between you and strengthen your role as pack leader.

Listed below are some things you may want to try. Those marked with an asterisk (*) are for developmentally mature Great Danes who have been certified sound for a particular activity by a veterinarian. They are NOT for puppies or adolescents whose bones and joints are still growing, nor are they for out-of-shape Danes or those that have bone or joint problems, heart disease or any other illness or infirmity that could be aggravated by heavy exercise.

SWIMMING: Swimming is a wonderful exercise for a Great Dane. You can get his heart pumping, work his muscles, and tire him out without stressing his bones and joints. Remember that wearing a life preserver is important for your Dane, just as it is for you.

Weather allowing, you can introduce your puppy to the water once his immunizations are complete. No matter what his age, introduce swimming gently and allow him to learn at his own pace. Never push or throw your dog into the water!

All training should be done in calm water. Begin by letting your dog explore around the water. Even if it takes several visits, wait until he begins to splash around in the

Siegreich Von Leben UD, TDI dons her life vest for an afternoon swim with Chris and Henry Bredenkamp, Siegreich Danes.

shallow water before encouraging him to go any further. As soon as he's in even an inch of water, praise him happily to build his confidence.

Toss a ball or other floating toy a few inches into the water. Encourage your dog to go after it, but never push him. If he's not ready yet, you go after it. He may come with you, but maybe not. Encourage and praise him; make it fun! Don't push or expect too much in any single session. Take your time and just enjoy your dog. Come the day that he willingly runs into the water after the ball, begin increasing the distance of your throw just a little bit at a time. The first time he goes in over his head, laugh and clap and tell him enthusiastically what a great dog he is! Don't worry if he does a lot of splashing; it takes time to become an accomplished swimmer! Don't overdo or tire him out at this point. Let him swim to retrieve his ball once or twice, then call it a day.

If you're stymied at some point—your dog doesn't go after the ball at all, perhaps—you can always wade in just a little and encourage him to follow, perhaps offering a small cookie or a favorite toy. Never force—make it fun and easy with small baby steps toward the ultimate goal. Eventually your Dane will be swimming like a champ!

CAUTION: Never leave your dog alone in the water. Never let him near a backyard pool or other body of water if you are unable to accompany and supervise him. If you have a pool, teach your dog where the steps are and how to get out. If you're swimming in a chlorinated pool or in salt water, watch his eyes for irritation and rinse the salt or chlorine from his coat and skin when you're finished. If your Dane is a good swimmer in calm water, don't assume he can navigate ocean waves. Introduce ocean swimming slowly, and ALWAYS supervise closely. Make sure when swimming together that your Dane does not try to climb or jump on you—you could easily drown! Remember, common sense is your best ally.

JUNIOR HANDLING: If you have a show quality Dane and a child 10 to 16 years of age, consider junior showmanship classes at your local dog training club. Many children enjoy working with the family dog, and this is an excellent way to increase your youngster's confidence and responsibility.

Lots of AKC dog shows have a Junior Handling Class. The judge picks a winner based not on the quality of the dog but on the child's ability to properly present the dog.

A Junior Handler is responsible for training his or her dog, and

Treasure Hauer, of Alpine, CA, handles O'Horcain's Tarzan II V. Hauer.

providing care and grooming. It's a great opportunity to support your child toward a goal and cheer him or her on.

At the same time, your child will have the opportunity to meet other youngsters, to learn sportsmanship, to bond with and be responsible for a pet, and to pick up valuable skills in organization, planning and record-keeping. Contact the AKC (see Appendix C) or your local breed or training club for more information.

HIKING*: Wilderness hiking with your healthy adult Dane can be great fun for both of you. There are, however, some very important guidelines that you should follow.

Make sure that the park or area where you will be hiking allows dogs. Unfortunately, many do not these days.

If you plan to have your dog carry a pack, begin preparing her way in advance. She can safely lug around 10-15 pounds if she's used to the pack and has been slowly conditioned with increasing weight until reaching a maximum load.

Your veterinarian should do a checkup to make sure Daisy's in shape for the trip. If all is well, ask for advice on any first-aid items to take along. You will probably need foot pad conditioner/protectant, scissors, tweezers, gauze, tape, styptic powder, antibiotic ointment, buffered aspirin and kaopectate. Make sure you know how to use all the supplies and medications, and in what dosage. Remember that up-to-date vaccinations and regular heartworm preventive are an absolute must. A snake bite kit would be an added plus for both you and your dog.

Condition Daisy in advance. A dog who typically jogs 15 minutes a day is not ready for an all-day hike! Choose a month with mild weather—not too hot and not too cold. Extremely cold weather and snow should be left for the Arctic breeds to enjoy—a Great Dane is not so well-protected by Mother Nature for wintery, inclement weather. And the hot summer sun is a potential hazard for any dog. Even if you will be hiking in fairly mild temperatures, ask

Daynakin's Blind Obsession CDX, TD sports a homemade back pack for her hikes with Marta Brock, of Rolling Thunder Danes.

your vet to discuss the signs of heat stress and what to do if your dog experiences any of them. Then avoid the possibility by providing frequent opportunities to drink water and to cool off and rest in the shade.

Take along plenty of fresh water for both of you. If you run short, don't allow your dog to drink any water from a river or stream without boiling it first. Many diseases lurk in unsterilized water.

Feed your Dane the same food she eats at home. Give small amounts three times a day and allow her to rest after eating. A dog biscuit now and then will be a welcome treat, but snacking on unfamiliar foods could affect her digestion.

Remember that the current in rushing water may be too strong for Daisy. Test the water before allowing her to cross a stream. Make sure you're not near a waterfall that could carry her over the edge, and always cross at the most shallow point.

Most insect repellants that you would buy for yourself contain deet, and are usually safe for a dog in small

Walhalla's Madam Butterfly CGC enjoys hiking. Owned by Chris and Henry Bredenkamp, Siegreich Danes, Burleson, Texas.

amounts. Still, make sure your vet approves the particular repellant you plan to use as safe for Daisy.

Brush her at the end of each day to dislodge any ticks before they burrow. Once you're home again, bathe for ticks and fleas with a flea shampoo obtained from your vet.

Last but not least, be prepared to clean up after your dog. Dog feces near streams and on trails can be a problem for other hikers. You might also ruin future opportunities for yourself and others to enjoy the wilderness with dogs. Too many inconsiderate owners and the "No Dogs Allowed" signs go up!

AGILITY*: Agility is an obstacle course for dogs. Some Danes may be too large for certain obstacles, and care must be taken to provide proper training and safety measures, especially if you intend to compete with such a large dog.

There are between 13 and 20 obstacles in a typical course, including an A-frame, see-saw, weave poles, and various jumps and tunnels. Your dog must complete each obstacle in course order, receiving faults if he misses an obstacle or takes it in the wrong direction, knocks a pole off a jump, or misses a yellow safety "contact" zone which must be touched on certain obstacles. You can direct your dog with commands and encouragements, but you cannot touch him or any of the obstacles during the competition. Scores are based on a combination of time and performance.

The AKC offers agility titles to dogs who earn a qualifying score of 85 out of a possible 100 on three occasions under a minimum of two judges. The difficulty of the course increases in each of four successive classes. Your Dane can become an NA (Novice Agility Dog), OA (Open Agility Dog), AX (Agility Dog Excellent) or an MX (Master Agility Excellent).

BICYCLING*: If you like to bike, let your healthy adult Dane join you. To run with a bike, the dog must be in excellent shape, properly conditioned and obedience trained.

Start with a physical exam, and ask your vet for tips on conditioning the body and toughening up the foot pads. There are specially designed bike attachments for running your dog securely leashed but out away from the wheels. Otherwise, consider a retractable leash, keeping in mind that they are not really designed to hold a pulling or

Marta Brock teaches Bumper (Can. Ch. Paquestone's V. Rolling Thunder CDX, TD, Can. CDX, TD, U-CD, ASCA-CD, WD, TDI) the A-Frame used in Agility.

misbehaving dog this big and strong. Your dog must be well-behaved and must enjoy the exercise.

Carry along an extra bottle of water for Rover. Don't allow him to gulp large amounts of water; frequent sips to keep him cool and hydrated are best. Do not offer food for at least an hour before and after strenuous exercise. Don't expect the dog to carry a pack or any extra weight while running, and never take him along when it's very hot and humid. Avoid concrete and asphalt surfaces as much as possible; flat, natural surfaces are safer and more comfortable for your dog.

Rover will need to warm up and cool down, just as you do. But even with proper preparation, don't overdo the exercise. A dog who wants to be with his master may continue to run long after his body says "stop," in an effort to please you. It's up to you to know when enough is enough. Biking through the neighborhood in the evenings is great; 10K runs are way, way too much. Even if Rover is in optimum condition, don't expect him to fly through the neighborhood at an all-out run. The best pace is a reasonable trot, starting with 5-10 minutes and working up to 20-30 minutes at a time, weather permitting. Just as with all other strenuous exercise, common sense is the key for both you and your dog.

FUN RUNS*: Human/canine fun runs are held in lots of cities, often as a fund raiser for animal shelters or other worthy causes. If you plan to participate with your Dane, follow the same fitness guidelines, conditioning requirements and precautions as detailed in the "BICYCLING" section above. As a matter of fact, having Rover jog beside a bicycle three or four times a week would be excellent preparation for fun run participation.

Most organized fun runs include a two-mile running course, plus a one-mile course for walkers and/or runners. The routes are carefully planned for the benefit of both man and dog. Most also have emergency "pit stops" should you or your dog become overheated or experience a minor injury. Joining a charity run is just one of several ways you can have fun with your dog and give to the community at the same time.

FRISBEE*: If your Dane is in shape and enjoys fetch, you can teach her to play frisbee with you. While she's still fairly young, you can begin tossing her one of the soft discs designed for dogs, but don't allow lots of running and jumping until her body is mature. Use the "come" command (See Chapter 22) to have her bring the disc back to you. If she doesn't want to return, reel her in with a long leash until she gets the idea. Be enthusiastic—it's a game and should be fun for both of you! Once she's older, you can use the more solid discs if you like. Teach her to run and catch by pointing her in the direction you'll be throwing, then tossing the disc for her to go after. Always remember—praise, praise, praise!

FLYBALL*: While a great many flyball dogs are sporting and herding breeds, there are a number of Great Danes across the country enjoying the sport and doing well

Black Zeus of T's Mist, owned by the author, is an enthusiastic frisbee player.

at it. Your Dane must be physically mature, in excellent shape, agile and trained in basic obedience. If he loves to play ball, enjoys being around other dogs and people, and likes to run and jump, you've found your perfect game!

What is flyball? It's a relay race between two teams, with four dogs on each team. The dogs are released one at a time to jump over four hurdles, step on a pedal on the flyball box to release a tennis ball, catch the ball and go back over the four hurdles. The fastest team to correctly complete the course wins the heat.

The height your dog will be jumping depends on the size of the smallest dog on his team. The minimum jump will be eight inches, the maximum 16 inches. Your dog will run 26 feet from the starting line to the first jump. There are ten feet between jumps, and the flyball box is 15 feet beyond the last jump.

The North American Flyball Association (See Appendix C) can provide you with complete instructions, training books and the names of training clubs in your area. Competitions are held across the country for dogs who do well in the sport, and points are awarded based on course completion times. Your Dane can earn a Flyball Dog (FD) or Flyball Dog Excellent (FDX) title, or perhaps even become a Flyball Dog Champion (FDCh).

If there are other dogs in your household that are healthy and active, train them all for a real family activity. They need not be purebred or registered to participate.

If you live in a rural area with no training clubs nearby, get together with some friends, set up a course in a big backyard and make it a neighborhood social event! Jumps and boxes can be ordered from many mail order supply companies (See Appendix C).

TRACKING*: While a hyperactive Dane might be great at flyball or frisbee, she's probably not the best tracking prospect. But if your Dane is fairly calm with a good attention span, is in sound shape and enjoys sniffing and retrieving, let her try tracking. This is a competitive sport for a dog/handler team, so both of you must enjoy trekking around in the great outdoors, over various types of terrain.

You can't force a dog to track, but most enjoy it if you train with an attitude of excitement and positive reinforcement. Without any training at all, the average dog uses his nose to "read" messages left by other dogs and to identify people. He can even smell when you are angry or afraid. You can begin scent discrimination training while Rover is still young if you use common sense—no long hikes or forced exercise, just hiding articles nearby and encouraging him to scent them out.

Supplies for tracking, such as a padded harness and extra-long leash, are available from many mail order companies (See Appendix C). Rules and regulations can be obtained from

Can. Ch. Paquestone's V. Rolling Thunder CDX, TD, Can. CDX, TD, U-CD, ASCA-CD, WD, TDI enjoys tracking.

the AKC. Your local obedience club can probably help you find a tracking group; if not, contact the AKC or NADOI (See Appendix C).

Tracking Dog (TD) and Tracking Dog Excellent (TDX) titles are given to dogs who pass the necessary AKC tracking tests.

CARTING*: Many Great Danes love to pull. Instead of letting him pull you down the street, why not teach him to pull a small cart or wagon? He must be fully developed,

healthy and sound, and trained in basic obedience before doing any actual harness work.

After you teach "Stand/stay" (See Chapter 22), use the same training principles to teach "Let's go," "back up" and "whoa." You can also begin to get your young Dane used to a well-fitted pulling harness, and even let him tug around a cardboard box with four little wheels attached! Just save the heavy work for your physically fit adult Dane. Even then, remember that this is for fun only—keep the weight to a minimum. He may be a very large dog, but he's not a pack horse!

Train slowly and patiently. It may take months before he pulls a cart loaded with the week's garbage from the garage to the curb. If you want Rover to look forward to pulling and to showing off his new skills, just take it one step at a time. If he's frightened or confused, you're moving too fast. With lots of love, praise, understanding and enthusiasm, you can teach your Dane to do this or almost anything! Harnesses, training books, cart building plans,

216

etc. are available from many mail order companies (See Appendix C). Rover can compete in draft tests if the two of you enjoy carting, or you can utilize his pulling skills for a number of activities designed for experienced pullers, such as weight pulling competitions, in-line skating with your Dane (no, HE doesn't wear the skates!), skijouring, where your Dane would provide the power to propel you as you snow-ski, or sledding. Appendix C lists organizations you can contact for additional information.

CAR TRAVEL: There's no reason your Dane can't join you on vacation, provided it's the right kind of vacation. Bus, train and plane trips are best done without your dog, as are trips where you'll be touring museums all day and dancing the night away. If your plans don't leave any time for your dog, hire a reputable pet sitter or board with your veterinarian or ABKA-approved boarding kennel (See Appendix C).

Rolls (Am. & Can. Ch. & O. T. Ch. Danehaven's Rolling Thunder UDT, Can. UDTDX, WDX, HC, U-CDX, TDI) pulls an incredible 5,100 pounds for owner Marta Brock.

CAUTION: Never leave your dog with anyone that you aren't POSITIVE you can trust! Look over the facilities, ask lots of questions, check references. While many kennels and pet-sitting companies are run by responsible, animal-loving people, many aren't. Dogs are mistreated, become ill and die under the supervision of "professional" pet sitters and boarding kennel personnel. If you have any doubts, don't leave your dog!

If you think your trip is one Rover will enjoy—say, early morning birdwatching, lounging by the pool, communing with Mother Nature—take him along! Make sure you have advance reservations at places where your dog is permitted. Your local library will have books to help you find lodging where pets are allowed (See Appendix C), but call ahead to make sure they have room for you, haven't changed their pet policy and understand that your

"Hang on, Mom!" Rolls and Ims (Daynakin's I'm a Rolling Thunder CDX, TD, Can. CD, TD, U-CD, WDX, HC, TDI) take Marta Brock skijorring.

particular pet is very large! Don't hesitate to tout your Dane's good points—obedience trained, crated when unsupervised, clean with no fleas—but be honest! Don't build a reputation you and Rover can't live up to. Then while you're in residence, keep him quiet and under control, and always clean up after him!

When you're on the road, keep your dog crated in the rear of your van or Suburban-type vehicle. Your Dane can travel in a car IF it's a large car and the back seat is all hers, but it's not as safe. Take along bedding, food and water from home, dishes and a first-aid kit. Make sure she has on both her permanent identification tags with your home address AND a temporary write-on tag with the address and phone number of your vacation residence.

NEVER let Daisy out of the vehicle without a leash. NEVER let her stick her head out a window while the vehicle is moving. NEVER leave her alone in a closed vehicle. Make safety your first priority, then relax and have a good time!

FUN AND GAMES: So you don't have a bike, or Rover hates the water, or Daisy will only track as far as her dinner bowl. Seems like the activities mentioned so far are just "not quite right" for the two of you? Can you still have fun together? You bet!

First of all, every dog should have toys available. Nylon bones are great for solo fun and they don't break or splinter. If you offer rawhide bones, do so ONLY when you can supervise, and make sure it's quality rawhide from the United States. Avoid plastic toys, and never buy those with removable squeakers. Sturdy vinyl and rubber toys and balls are great fun; make sure that pieces are not being chewed off and that the toy is too big to be swallowed.

Now put those toys to use! Hide the rubber ducky behind the tree and let Rover "go find it;" play fetch in the backyard with a tennis ball. Teach Daisy to "catch" the rubber dumbbell. Take out a soccer ball and encourage her

Marta Brock's Rolling Thunder Danes follow her Samoyed lead dog.

to bat it around with her muzzle and feet—the two of you will soon be playing soccer!

When it's hot outside, run through the sprinklers together, or splash around in a wading pool. Jump in piles of leaves in the fall. Take nature walks in the spring. Teach Rover to help carry in firewood in the winter. Make it a game to put his doggie toys back in the toy box; teach him to bring in the newspaper every day, or the mail. You can even teach him to pick up the towels that the kids leave all over the bathroom floor—just open the hamper and have him toss them in!

Have someone hold Daisy while you hide, then send her to find you. Until she learns the game, encourage her with "Over here, Daisy. Here I am." Give her a hug and a small treat when she finds you.

Play the shell game, hiding treats under overturned bowls and encouraging Rover to "find it." Make it obvious at first— soon you'll be able to mix up

Danes love to play. Sharpening his soccor skills is Marta Brock's Rolls.

220

six or seven bowls and he'll sniff out the treat.

Play tag. Teach Daisy to sing harmony with you. Take her to visit other dogs in the neighborhood. Throw a "puppy party" on her birthday. Put horns on her head at Halloween and take her trick-or-treating, as long as she's not shy or easily frightened.

Use your imagination, with a healthy dose of common sense. Your dog will feel very loved and secure, and he'll wag his tail a lot. And every time that tail starts to wag real hard, you'll find yourself starting to smile—automatically! Your blood pressure will decrease; you'll catch fewer colds; you'll feel less stressed. It's true! The more you love and cherish and have fun with this beautiful, marvelous dog, the healthier and happier you'll both be! Wow, are you lucky—THAT'S A GREAT DOG!!!

A Great Dane herding sheep? Marta Brock's Am. & Can. Ch. & O.T. Ch. Danehaven's Rolling Thunder UDT, Can. UDTDX, WDX, HC, U-CDX, TDI proves that Danes can do anything!

Am. & Can. Ch. and O.T. Ch. Danehaven's Rolling Thunder UDT, Can. UDTDX, WDX, HC, U-CDX, TDI and Daynakin's I'm a Rolling Thunder CDX TD, Can. CD, TD, U-CD, WDX, HC, TDI owned by Marta Brock, Rolling Thunder Danes, Olympia, Washington.

APPENDIX A

Official AKC Standard

General Appearance—The Great Dane combines, in its regal appearance, dignity, strength and elegance with great size and a powerful, well-formed, smoothly muscled body. It is one of the giant working breeds, but is unique in that its general conformation is so well balanced that it never appears clumsy, and shall move with a long reach and powerful drive. It is always a unit—the Apollo of dogs. A Great Dane must be spirited, courageous, never timid: always friendly and dependable. This physical and mental combination is the characteristic which gives the Great Dane the majesty possessed by no other breed. It is particularly true of this breed that there is an impression of great masculinity in dogs, as compared to an impression of femininity in bitches. Lack of true Dane breed type, as defined in this standard, is a serious fault.

Size, Proportion, Substance—The male should appear more massive throughout than the bitch, with larger frame and heavier bone. In the ratio between length and height, the Great Dane should be square. In bitches, a somewhat longer body is permissible, providing she is well proportioned to her height. Coarseness or lack of substance are equally undesirable. The male shall not be less than 30 inches at the shoulders, but it is preferable that he be 32 inches or more, providing he is well proportioned to his height. The female shall not be less than 28 inches at the shoulders, but it is preferable that she be 30 inches or more, providing she is well proportioned to her height. Danes under the minimum height must be disqualified.

Head—The head shall be rectangular, long, distinguished, expressive, finely chiseled, especially below the eyes. Seen from the side, the Dane's forehead must be sharply set off from the bridge of the nose, (a strongly pronounced stop). The plane of the skull and the plane of the muzzle must slope without any bony protuberance in a smooth line to a full square jaw with a deep muzzle (fluttering flews are undesirable). The masculinity of the male is very pronounced in structural appearance of the head. The bitch's head is more delicately formed. Seen from the top, the skull should have parallel sides and the bridge of the nose should be as broad as possible. The cheek muscles should not be prominent. The length from the tip of the nose to the center of the stop should be equal to the length from the center of the stop to the rear of the slightly developed occiput. The head should be angular from all sides and should have flat planes with dimensions in proportion to the size of the Dane. Whiskers may be trimmed or left natural.

Eyes shall be medium size, deep set, and dark, with a lively intelligent expression. The eyelids are almond-shaped and relatively tight, with well developed brows. Haws and Mongolian eyes are serious faults. In harlequins, the eyes should be dark; light colored eyes, eyes of different colors and walleyes are permitted but not desirable.

Ears shall be high set, medium in size and of moderate thickness, folded forward close to the cheek. The top line of the folded ear should be level with the skull. If cropped, the ear length is in proportion to the size of the head and the ears are carried uniformly erect.

Nose shall be black, except in the blue Dane, where it is a dark blue-black. A black spotted nose is permitted in the harlequin; a pink colored nose is not desirable. A split nose is a disqualification.

Teeth shall be strong, well developed, clean and with full dentition. The incisors of the lower jaw touch very lightly the bottoms of the inner surface of the upper incisors (scissors bite). An undershot jaw is a very serious fault. Overshot or wry bites are serious faults. Even bites, misaligned or crowded incisors are minor faults.

Neck, Topline, Body—The neck shall be firm, high set, well arched, long and muscular. From the nape it should gradually broaden and flow smoothly into the withers. The neck underline should be clean.

Withers shall slope smoothly into a short level back with a broad loin. The chest shall be broad, deep and well muscled. The forechest should be well developed without a pronounced sternum. The brisket extends to the elbow, with well sprung ribs. The body underline should be tightly muscled with a well-defined tuck-up.

The croup should be broad and very slightly sloping. The tail should be set high and smoothly into the croup, but not quite level with the back, a continuation of the spine. The tail should be broad at the base, tapering uniformly down to the hock joint. At rest, the tail should fall straight. When excited or running, it may curve slightly, but never above the level of the back. A ring or hooked tail is a serious fault. A docked tail is a disqualification.

Forequarters—The forequarters, viewed from the side, shall be strong and muscular. The shoulder blade must be strong and sloping, forming, as near as possible, a right angle in its articulation with the upper arm. A line from the upper tip of the shoulder to the back of the elbow joint should be perpendicular. The ligaments and muscles holding the shoulder blade to the rib cage must be well developed, firm and securely attached to prevent loose shoulders. The shoulder blade and the upper arm should be the same length. The elbow should be one-half the distance from the withers to the ground. The strong pasterns should slope slightly. The feet should be round and compact with well-arched toes, neither toeing in, toeing out, nor rolling to the inside or outside. The nails should be short, strong and as dark as possible, except that they may be lighter in harlequins. Dewclaws may or may not be removed.

Hindquarters—The hindquarters shall be strong, broad, muscular and well angulated, with well let down hocks. Seen from the rear, the hock joints appear to be perfectly straight, turned neither toward the inside nor toward the outside. The rear feet should be round and compact, with well-arched toes, neither toeing in nor out. The nails should be short, strong and as dark as possible, except they may be lighter in harlequins. Wolf claws are a serious fault.

Coat—The coat shall be short, thick and clean with a smooth glossy appearance.

Color, Markings and Patterns—*Brindle*— The base color shall be yellow gold and always brindled with strong black cross stripes in a chevron pattern. A black mask is preferred. Black should appear on the eye rims and eyebrows, and may appear on the ears and tail tip. The more intensive the base color and the more distinct and even the brindling, the more preferred will be the color. Too much or too little brindling are equally undesirable. White markings at the chest and toes, black-fronted dirty colored brindles are not desirable.

Fawn— The color shall be yellow gold with a black mask. Black should appear o the eye rims and eyebrows, and may appear on the ears and tail tip. The deep yellow gold must always be given the preference. White markings at the chest and toes, black fronted, dirty colored fawns are not desirable.

Blue— The color shall be a pure steel blue. White markings at the chest and toes are not desirable.

Black— The color shall be a glossy black. White markings at the chest and toes are not desirable.

Harlequin— Base color shall be pure white with black torn patches irregularly and well distributed over the entire body; a pure white neck is preferred. The black patches should never be large enough to give the appearance of a blanket, nor so small as to give a stippled or dappled effect. Eligible, but less desirable, are a few small gray patches, or a white base with single black hairs showing through, which tend to give a salt and pepper or dirty effect.

Any variance in color or markings as described above shall be faulted to the extent of the deviation. Any Great Dane which does not fall within the above color classifications must be disqualified.

Gait—The gait denotes strength and power with long, easy strides resulting in no tossing, rolling or bouncing of the topline or body. The backline shall appear level and parallel to the ground. The long reach should strike the ground below the nose while the head is carried forward. The powerful rear drive should be balanced to the reach. As speed increases, there is a natural tendency for the legs to converge toward the centerline of balance beneath the body. There should be no twisting in or out at the elbow or hock joints.

Temperament—The Great Dane must be spirited, courageous, always friendly and dependable, and never timid or aggressive.

DISQUALIFICATIONS

Danes under minimum height.
Split nose.
Docked tail.
Any color other than those described under "Color, Markings and Patterns."

Approved 1990

OFFICIAL UKC STANDARD

(Guardian Dogs Group)

HISTORY

The Great Dane is a mastiff type. Nearly every country in Europe and Asia have examples of this type of dog. The breed, or its ancestors, date back hundreds of years, but Germany lays claim for the modern development of the breed. By 1880 a breed standard was agreed upon. It was 1900 before the breed was imported to Britain.

The Great Dane has been recognized by the United Kennel Club since 1923.

GENERAL APPEARANCE

A large dog, often reaching 36 inches at the withers, with a long tail and cropped or uncropped ears. Its short, smooth coat comes in brindle, black, blue, fawn and harlequin colors. It should be as square as possible in relation of height to length.

CHARACTERISTICS

The Great Dane is active and affectionate to its owners. It can be a very imposing guard dog, as its history relates, but is quite easily trained. The breed does require room and exercise.

HEAD & SKULL

The head, taken together, should give the impression of great length and strength of jaw. It has a strongly pronounced stop. The skull should be flat and have a slight indentation running up the center, the occipital peak is not prominent. The bridge of the nose should be very wide, with a slight ridge where the cartilage joins the bone. The nostrils should be large, wide and open, giving a blunt look to the nose. Masculinity of the males is pronounced in the expression and structure of the head; femininity of the females is likewise evident.

NOSE—The nose is black, except in harlequins, where a black spotted nose is permitted.

EYES—Medium in size, and as dark as possible; with almond-shaped eyelids. Eyebrows are well developed.

EARS—Set high. Cropped or uncropped. (Cropping is becoming less desirable for humane and health reasons.) When cropped, they are well pointed and in proportion to the head. If left natural, the ears are of moderate size and thickness, dropping forward close to the neck.

TEETH—A full compliment of strong, white teeth meet in a scissors bite.

Faults—Even bite, undershot, overshot. Missing teeth, Incisors out of line.

NECK

The neck is firm and clean, high-set, well-arched, long, sinewy and muscular.

FOREQUARTERS

The shoulders are muscular and well sloped back, with the elbows well under the body. The legs are straight, strong and muscular. The pasterns slope only slightly forward.

BODY

Chest is very deep and broad, with a tuck up. The ribs are well sprung. The withers are the highest part of the back, which slopes slightly toward the loins with a very slight arch.

HINDQUARTERS

Hindquarters and thighs should be extremely muscular, giving the idea of great strength. The stifle and hock are well bent, turning neither in nor out.

FEET

Round and turned neither in nor out. The toes are short, highly-arched and well closed. The nails are as dark as possible.

TAIL

Should start high and fairly broad, terminating slender and thin at the level of the hock joint. When the dog is running or excited, the tail is slightly curved.

COLOR

Black, brindle, blue, fawn and harlequin.

COAT

The hair is short and dense, and sleek-looking.
Fault—Coat coarse to the touch.

SIZE

Adult males—not less than 30" at the withers, 32" and over being preferable.
Adult females—not be less than 28", with 30" and over being preferable. The average weight of an adult male is 120 pounds, and of a female is 100 pounds.

DISQUALIFICATIONS

Under minimum height. Albinos, merles. Docked tails. Split noses. Unilateral or bilateral cryptorchid. Extreme viciousness or shyness. These disqualifications are so serious to the breed that dogs with these faults should not be used for breeding.

Copyright 1991

APPENDIX B

Code of Ethics

This Code is established in accordance with the objectives of the GDCA to protect and advance the interests of Great Danes, and to provide guidelines for responsible ownership and ethical breeding practices.

ALL MEMBERS SHALL:

- Maintain the best possible standards of health, cleanliness, safety, and care of their dogs.
- Take all appropriate measures to assist a Dane in distress.
- Display good sportsmanship and conduct, whether at home, at shows, or in hotels, in such a manner as to reflect credit upon themselves and the GDCA.
- Not alter the appearance, physical structure, condition, or natural temperament of a dog by any means other than allowed for in the Official Breed Standard if the dog is to exhibited.
- Bear the responsibility for the truth and accuracy of any information and/or photographs submitted for publication.

ALL BREEDERS AND OWNERS OF GREAT DANES (BITCHES AND STUD DOGS ALIKE) SHALL:

1. Breed Great Danes which are temperamentally and structurally sound.
2. Be familiar with the Breed Standard and breed only those dogs and bitches which most closely conform to it.
3. Keep well informed in the field of genetics and work to eliminate hereditary defects from the breed.
4. Refrain from further use of a Great Dane for breeding if the dog or bitch has produced any offspring with serious inherited defects detrimental to the animal's well being (physically or mentally), and had produced like results with a different mating partner.
5. Not breed to an unregistered Great Dane.
6. Not wholesale litters of Great Danes, sell to Brokers or Pet Shops, provide any animal for prize or raffle purposes; nor use a Stud Dog in like manner.
7. Keep all puppies with the litter until at least 7 or 8 weeks of age.
8. Adhere to State and Local laws regarding the sale of puppies.
9. Sell dogs in good condition, health, and sound temperament at time

of delivery. They shall be free of internal parasites to the best knowledge of the seller; will have received the necessary inoculations to date; a record of dates and types of immunizations will be given; and a health certificate provided if required. Written instructions on the feeding, health care, training, and any other information necessary for the dog's well being (e.g. ear crop care), will be made available after the sale to assist the new owner.

10. Provide a four or more generation color marked pedigree and the AKC registration at the time of sale of each dog. Any dog sold as a pet and not for breeding should be given a limited registration or a written contract specifying conditions of sale (e.g. spay/neuter agreement, show or pet quality, co-ownership, breeding rights, etc.)

11. Provide the buyer with copies of all pre-screenings done on both parents to assure the buyer that every possible effort has been made to produce puppies free of hereditary problems.

12. Sell or place each Great Dane with the contemplated final owner, therefore the seller should ascertain that the prospective buyer has the knowledge and facilities to properly care for a growing or grown dog. As a condition of sale or placement, the breeder shall retain the first right of refusal should the purchaser ever decide to transfer ownership or resell the dog, therefore giving the seller every opportunity to help the purchaser find a new home for the dog if necessary.

13. All dogs sold (puppy or adult) shall have a signed agreement between the seller and purchaser that the animal shall be examined by a Veterinarian of the purchaser's choice (and paid for by that party), within 72 hours of purchase or delivery. If the dog is deemed unhealthy or possessing an inherited defect which would impair the use for which it was purchased (pet, show, or breeding program), the seller shall refund the full purchase price upon the return of the dog with a Veterinarian certified documentation of the condition. The dog will be returned at the purchaser's expense.

14. Use only the agreed upon Stud Dog at a breeding in the absence of the owner of the Bitch.

15. Provide and honor all contracts regarding sales, co-ownerships, breeding rights, agreements, compensation for future puppies, leasing a bitch, stud service, etc.

IT IS STRONGLY RECOMMENDED THAT:

1. All dogs and bitches to be bred be x-rayed prior to breeding and declared free of hip dysplasia by a knowledgeable Veterinarian or the OFA. It is also encouraged that any and all technology available

be used to screen all animals to be used for breeding, according to known problems within the breed (e.g. OFA, cardiac check, thyroid check, VWD, PRA, etc.)

2. A written Stud Contract be used which specifies all conditions of the breeding, and a color marked pedigree be provided by both parties.

3. A stud dog should be a year or more before breeding, and a bitch not less than 18 months.

4. A bitch not be bred more than once a year.

5. Both parties provide Veterinarian reports certifying that each animal is clear of any transmittable infections.

6. With the agreement of both the seller and the purchaser, any puppy sold as a show prospect which subsequently develops a disqualifying defect shall be:

a. replaced by the breeder with another show prospect puppy and the dog returned to the seller, OR

b. the money refunded and the dog returned to the seller, OR

c. the buyer's money refunded to the extent of the difference between the price paid and the price of the pet puppies sold from the same or similar litters if the buyer retains and spays or neuters the dog.

7. Breeders adhere to the GDCA Breeders Color Code.

Code of Ethics Committee
Co-Chairpeople: Clare Lincoln and Margaret Shappard
       Members: Karla Callahan
                      Anita Dunne
                      Col. Harry Hutchinson
                      Marilyn Riggins
                      Terri Welti

Breeders Color Code

as endorsed by

The Great Dane Club of America

There are only five recognized colors; all these basically fall into four color strains. 1. FAWN and BRINDLE, 2. HARLEQUIN and HARLEQUIN BRED BLACK, 3. BLUE and BLUE BRED BLACK, 4. BLACK. Color classifications being well founded, the Great Dane Club of America, Inc. considers it an advisable practice to mix color strains and it is the club's policy to adhere only to the following breedings:

Color of Dane	*Approved Breedings*	*Desired Pedigrees*
1. FAWN	1. FAWN bred to FAWN or BRINDLE only	Pedigrees of FAWN or BRINDLE Danes *should not* carry BLACK, HARLE-QUIN or BLUE upon them.
1. BRINDLE	1. BRINDLE bred to BRINDLE or FAWN only	
2. HARLEQUIN	2. HARLEQUIN bred to HARLEQUIN breeding or BLACK from BLACK BREED-ING only	Pedigrees of HARLE-QUIN or HARLE-QUIN BRED BLACK Danes *should not* carry FAWN, BRINDLE or BLUE upon them.
2. BLACK (HARLEQUIN BRED)	BLACK from HARLE-QUIN BREEDING bred to HARLEQUIN, BLACK from HARLE-QUIN BREEDING or BLACK from BLACK BREEDING ONLY	
3. BLUE	3. BLUE bred to BLUE, BLACK from BLUE BREEDING or BLACK from BLACK breeding only	Pedigrees of BLUE or BLUE BRED BLACK Danes *should not* carry FAWN, BRINDLE or HARLEQUIN upon them.
3. BLACK (BLUE BRED)	3. BLACK from BLUE BREEDING bred to BLUE, BLACK from BLUE BREEDING or BLACK from BLACK BREEDING ONLY	
4. BLACK (BLACK BRED)	4. BLACK from BLACK BREEDING bred to BLACK, BLUE or HARLEQUIN only (see note below)	Pedigrees of BLACK BRED Danes *should not* carry FAWN, BRINDLE, HAR-LEQUIN or BLUE upon them

NOTE: Black Bred Great Danes may be bred to Blacks, Blues or Harlequins only. Puppies resulting from these breedings will become Blacks or Harlequins from Harlequin breeding (category 2 above), Blacks or Blues from Blue breeding category (category 3 above) or Blacks from Black Breeding (category 4 above.)

IT SHALL BE THE GOAL OF ALL TO BREED FORWARD, NEVER BACKWARDS, TO ATTAIN PEDIGREES OF PUPPIES WHICH HAVE THE DESIRED COLOR STRAINS ENDORSED BY THE GREAT DANE CLUB OF AMERICA.

APPENDIX C - RESOURCES

ACTIVITY GROUPS/INFORMATION

Clever Canine Companions; 140 Weidler Ln.; Rothville, PA 18543.

Come 'N Get It Canine Frisbee Championship; P. O. Box 16279; Encino, CA 91416.

Delta Society Therapy Association; P. O. Box 1080; Renton, WA 98057-1080.

International Federation of Sled Dog Sports; 7118 N. Beehive Rd.; Pocatello, ID 83201.

International Sled Dog Racing Association; P. O. Box 446; Norman, ID 83848-0446.

International Weight Pull Association; 3455 Railroad Ave.; Post Falls, ID 83854; 310-364-1214.

Love-on-a-Leash Therapy Group; 3809 Plaza Dr. #107-309; Oceanside, CA 92056.

National Committee For Dog Agility; 401 Bluemont Circle; Manhattan, KS 66052.

North American Flyball Association; 1 Gooch Park Dr.; Barrie, Ontario L4M 4S6; Canada.

North American Skijor & Ski Pulk Association; 907-561-6111.

Owner Handler Association; P. O. Box 133; Ottsville, PA 18942; 215-847-2229.

Therapy Dogs Inc.; P. O. Box 2786; Cheyenne, WY 82003-2786; 307-638-3223.

Therapy Dogs International; 260 Fox Chase Rd.; Chester, NJ 07930.

US Dog Agility Association; P. O. Box 850955; Richardson, TX 75085-0955.

BOARDING KENNELS/PET SITTER REFERRALS

American Boarding Kennel Association; 4575 Galley Rd. #400A; Colorado Springs, CO 80915.

Pet Sitters International; 418 E. King St.; King, NC 27021; 800-268-7487.

Pet Sitting Referral Service; P. O. Box 619; Middletown, NJ 07748.

DOG OWNERS ASSOCIATIONS

American Dog Owners Association; 1654 Columbia Turnpike; Castleton, NY 12033.

Dog Fanciers Club; RD 2 Box 496; Flemington, NJ 08822.

Responsible Dog Owners Association; 242 Chapman Rd.; Doylestown, PA 18901.

Responsible Pet Owners Alliance; P. O. Box 701132; San Antonio, TX 78270; 210-695-3388.

GROOMER REFERRALS

National Dog Groomers Association of America; P. O. Box 101; Clark, PA 16113.

HANDLER REFERRALS

Dog Handlers' Guild; 5390 Irene Rd.; Belvidere, IL 61008.

Professional Handlers Association; 15810 Mount Everest Ln.; Silver Spring, MD 20906.

MAIL ORDER CATALOGS/SUPPLIES/EQUIPMENT

Big Dog Basics & Beyond; P. O. Box 1132C; Garden City, KS 67846.

Care-A-Lot; 1617 Diamond Springs Rd.; Virginia Beach, VA 23455; 804-460-9771.

Drs. Foster & Smith; 2253 Air Park Rd.; Box 100; Rhinelander, WI 54501-0100; 800-562-7169.

234

Healthy Tek Inc. nutritional supplements; 800-937-1104.

Holistic Pet Center; 800-788-7387.

Ikon Outfitters Limited; 7597 Latham Rd.; Lodi, WI 53555.

JB Pet Supplies; 5 Raritan Rd.; Oakland, NJ 07436; 800-526-0388.

Jeffers; P. O. Box 100; Dothan, AL 36305; 800-JEFFERS.

KV Vet Supply; P. O. Box 245; David City, NE 68632; 402-367-6047.

Mail Order Pet Shop; 1338 N. Market Blvd.; Sacramento, CA 95834; 800-366-7387.

Merion Station Mail Order; P. O. Box 100; Merion Station, PA 19066; 800-333-TAGS.

Morrills' New Directions natural care items & nutritional supplements; P. O. Box 30; Orient, ME 04471; 800-368-5057.

Natural Animal; P. O. Box 1177; St. Augustine, FL 32085; 800-274-7387.

Nordkin Outfitters; P. O. Box 1023; Graham, WA 98338-1023.

Orthomolecular Specialties; P. O. Box 32232; San Jose, CA 95152-2232; 408-227-9334.

Pedigrees; P. O. Box 905; Brockport, NY 14420; 800-437-8434.

Pet Warehouse; P. O. Box 310; Xenia, OH 45385; 800-443-1160.

R C Steele; P. O. Box 910; Brockport, NY 14420; 800-468-8781.

UPCO; P. O. Box 969; St. Joseph, MO 64502; 816-233-8800.

Valley Vet Supply; Box 504 Dept. P; Marysville, KS 66508; 800-531-2390.

Vet Vax Inc.; Box 4001 Dept. 101; Tonganoxie, KS 66086; 913-845-3760.

Wholesale Pet USA; 975 Ford St.; Colorado Springs, CO 80915; 800-444-0404.

MISCELLANEOUS INFORMATION

American Rescue Dog Association; P. O. Box 151; Chester, NY 10918.

Animal Behaviorist Society; Dept. of Psychology; Mercer University; 1400 Coleman Ave.; Macon, GA 31207.

Association of Obedience Clubs & Judges; 4869 Avoca Ave.; Ellicott City, MD 21043.

Camp Gone To The Dogs; RR 1 Box 958; Putney, VT 05346.

National Animal Poison Control Center; 800-548-2423 (credit card); 900-680-0000 (phone bill).

National 4H Council; 7100 Connecticut Ave.; Chevy Chase, MD 20815.

Touring With Towser Guide; Gaines Professional Services; P. O. Box 877; Young America, MN 55399.

PUBLICATIONS/MAGAZINES

Bloodlines Magazine; UKC; 100 E. Kilgore Rd.; Kalamazoo, MI 49001-5598.

Dane World; 92 Sachem St.; Middleboro, MA 02346; 508-947-3828.

Dog Fancy Magazine; P. O. Box 53264; Boulder, CO 80322-3264; 303-786-2306.

Dog Gone newsletter; P. O. Box 651155; Vero Beach, FL 32965-1155.

Dogs In Canada Magazine; 43 Railside Rd.; Don Mills, Ontario, M3A 3L9; Canada.

Dog World Magazine; 29 N. Wacker Dr.; Chicago, IL 60606-3298; 312-726-2802.

Front & Finish Magazine; P. O. Box 333; Galesburg, IL 61402.

Good Dog! Magazine; P. O. Box 31292; Charleston, SC 29417; 803-763-8750.

Great Dane Quarterly; 811 Spring St. #125; Paso Robles, CA 93446; 805-239-8406.

Great Dane Reporter; P. O. Box 5284; Beverly Hills, CA 90209.

Natural Pet Holistic Newsletter; P. O. Box 22899; Melbourne, FL 32902-2899; 407-723-4183.

Offlead Magazine; 100 Bouck St.; Rome, NY 13440.

Pure Bred Dogs/American Kennel Gazette; AKC; 51 Madison Ave.; New York, NY 10010

Wolf Clan Holistic Magazine; 3952 N. Southport Ave. #122; Chicago, IL 60613; 312-935-1000.

REGISTRIES/CLUBS

American Kennel Club; 51 Madison Ave.; New York, NY 10010. 5580 Centerview Dr.; Raleigh, NC 27606. Breeder Referral Service/Info Line - 900-407-7877. Anti-Dog Legislation Hotline - 800-AKC-TELL.

Canadian Kennel Club; 89 Skyway Ave.; Etobicoke, Ontario M9W 6R4; Canada.

Great Dane Club of America; Marie A. Fint, Secretary; 442 Country View Lane; Garland, TX 75043; 214-279-1016. GDCA Rescue - 203-272-8292.

United Kennel Club; 100 E. Kilgore Rd.; Kalamazoo, MI 49001.

TATTOO REGISTRIES

National Dog Registry; P. O. Box 116; Woodstock, NY 12498; 800-NDR-DOGS.

Tatoo-A-Pet; 1625 Emmons Ave.; Brooklyn, NY 11235.

TRAINER REFERRALS

National Association of Dog Obedience Instructors; 2286 E. Steel Rd.; St. Johns, MI 48879.

Society of North American Dog Trainers; ASPCA Companion Animal Services; 441 E. 92nd St.; New York, NY 10128; 212-243-5460.

VETERINARY REFERRALS/ ALTERNATIVE THERAPIES

American Animal Hospital Association; P. O. Box 150899; Denver, CO 80215-0899.

American Holistic Veterinary Medical Association; 2214 Old Emmorton Rd.; Bel Air, MD 21014.

American Veterinary Medical Association; 930 N. Meacham Rd.; Schaumburg, IL 60196.

International Veterinary Acupuncture Society; RD 4 Box 216; Chester Springs, PA 19425.

National Center For Homeopathy; 801 N. Fairfax #306; Alexandria, VA 22314.